Christian Faith in the 21st Century

Rev. Dr. Wayne R. Viereck

Dedication

Here I go again. After I had finished writing my book, "Then is Now: Reading the New Testament in the 21st Century," I thought I was done. Then the community of faith I am currently serving, in a retirement community in SaddleBrooke, Arizona, said, "Don't quit now!"

They asked me to write a book which would deal with the core issues of the Christian faith from the perspective of the 21st century. So here it is, with thanks to the many who have touched my life, changed me, loved me and enabled me to write this.

Most of all, I dedicate this book to the love of my life, my wife Pat. It was her encouragement that kept this book from ending on page one. And it is her editing and advice that has made this book better than it would have been.

So this is to you, Pat, my love, my inspiration, my editor and my greatest blessing.

Tucson Arizona
2021

Foreword

Sadly, Wayne Viereck, our husband, father, and friend passed away before he was able to publish this book. We, who love him, felt his words were important and needed to be shared with anyone seeking deeper understanding of their Christian Faith. We publish this book in his honor, and in gratitude for the many ways his words continue to guide us.

The Family of Wayne Viereck
Tucson Arizona
2022

Table of Contents

1. Philosophical Proofs for the Existence of God
2. Does God Exist?
3. The Existence of God is an Enigma
4. Revelation is Absolutely Necessary
5. Creation in the Secular World
6. Creation in the Christian Faith
7. The Origin of Life on Earth
8. The Church
9. Baptism
10. The Holy Spirit
11. Holy Communion…The Lord's Supper
12. Hell
13. Who Will Go to Hell?
14. Purgatory
15. Heaven
16. Eternal Life
17. Sin…Original Sin…Evil
18. Atonement
19. The End of the World
20. The Trinity
21. The Apostles Creed
22. The Lord's Prayer
23. Other Religions
24. Judaism
25. Islam

26. Hindus and Buddhists
27. Mormons
28. Atheism…Agnosticism…Secularism
29. LGBTQ

Reprise

About the Author

Preface

This is a book about the Christian Faith as understood in the 21st century. It is needed because, while the Faith does not change from previous centuries, the way in which it is best understood and the way it can best be expressed does change, just as the world's views of almost everything also changes.

Before we begin however, we should first ask "What is faith?" The writer of Hebrews tells us, "Now faith is the assurance of things hoped for, the conviction of things not seen" (Hebrews 11:2); another way to say that is, faith is to believe "nevertheless."

There are very few things in life about which there is absolute certainty and that is true of faith. Faith is to know that nevertheless, anyhow, in spite of when we are not certain, even when the fog is so thick we can't see beyond the next 5 minutes, God is there for us.

Faith is to know, in whatever situation in which we find ourselves, God's love surrounds us, and his grace upholds us. To be able, even in the midst of the pain, confusion, and uncertainty of life, to say "nevertheless" is what faith is all about. The Greek man, who said to Jesus, "Lord I believe ... help my unbelief!" is a brother to us all. We have been there, if not today we may be there tomorrow. We believe but we don't believe...or we are not all that sure what we believe. And what we believe today with passion may very well change as we experience new depths and nuances in life.

Actually, it is not our faith that changes so much as our understanding of our faith. That is the reason for this book....to look at the nuances and deeper possibilities which the 21st Century shows us about faith and having faith.

The Christian Faith is the answer to what are called "existential questions," those questions which remain as vital today as ever in human history; the meaning of existence, why there is death, what my responsibilities are in life, what is the meaning of my life?

Those are such incredibly important concerns; lack of answer to them can result in debilitating anguish, despair, mental illness or even suicide.

In the 21st Century we are slowly beginning to realize that apart from faith there is no satisfactory answer to the deep questions of life. Without faith we have only the flippant cynicism of, "Eat, drink and be merry for tomorrow we die," or the lying bravado of "who cares?" Well, the Christian faith assures us that God cares, and to know that is to have faith.

God cares so much that the fundamental assertion of the Christian faith is that God has come among us in the historical person, the real and true human being, Jesus of Nazareth. And in doing that…coming into human history, being incarnate in Jesus, God bound himself to human history and to that person Jesus. Therefore, God is not to be fully found anywhere else, not in abstract philosophy, material realism, theoretical or quantum physics, or any other place. We meet God only in human history, and in that history, God is fully revealed only in the historical person of Jesus.

Christianity is ever relevant to human living because the truth is that the more things change, the more they do not change at all; and the problems and difficulties which faced our ancestors face us still today. It was their faith that gave them the strength and power to endure and conquer. So also today, so also for us!

To live in faith is to live knowing that we matter, that our lives matter, that what we do matters, that it does make a difference. Not because our deeds will redeem the world, but because in Jesus Christ, God has already redeemed the world, abolished death, given dignity and meaning and purpose to life.

This is a truth which will remain true in spite of those who seek to degrade it, demean it or destroy it. As Christians we live in that faith. St. Paul says; "...not ashamed of the gospel, not with timid spirit, but with a spirit of power and love and self-control."

That's what this book is all about.

1

Philosophical Proofs for the Existence of God

We begin with something which is not at all part of the Christian faith but which needs to be considered because, while Christianity confidently asserts that, "In the beginning God created the heaven and the earth," this assertion brings forth from the secular world hoots of mocking derision, denial and rejection.

Ah, but always in every age there have been and still are some who are more discerning, more open to spiritual reality in the world and do not so quickly shut their minds. Intrigued by the possibility, perhaps even probability, that God does exist and does have interest in human affairs, many have undertaken a variety of efforts to prove God can be known and understood apart from relying upon faith and religion and without the need for the supernatural intervention of the Holy Spirit.

We look next at four of the most popular of these non-religious efforts, all of which in varying degrees are considered to be "reasonable" proofs for the existence of God. They are sophisticated philosophical efforts which try to seriously argue the existence of God as a sensible conclusion apart from revelation.

In the end, though, whether those efforts convince, or whether they fall short, they have nothing to do with the Christian faith. They are included because they are of historical importance and are sometimes confused with the Christian Faith. So we must at least briefly consider them.

The first argument: the Cosmological Proof

Way back in the 4th century B.C. Plato and Aristotle maintained that everything that is must have a cause which brought it into existence. That is except the "first cause" which Aristotle termed the "uncaused cause." Thomas Aquinas in his Summa Theologica (13th century) developed this argument into a logical proof that God must exist because the universe exists which required a causative act to get it going. He termed that cause God.

Then in the 18th century the philosopher Gottfried Leibniz developed this idea into the "Principle of Sufficient Reason." It is a beautifully complex agreement with Plato and Aristotle that "nothing can exist without sufficient reason for its existence."

Since the universe exists, the sufficient reason must be that God caused it to exist. Well, that would be a sufficient reason alright, but while it was good enough for its time, modern physics simply gives this argument an indulgent smile.

The second argument: the Teleological Proof

This view is derived from the Greek word "telos" which means the end purpose or goal of something. The argument says that since the universe exists there must be a reason why it exists. If there is no reason for it to exist then why does it exist? It would not. And if there is a reason or a purpose for the universe, then there must also be a creator who determined what that purpose would be. And, since it is impossible to believe there is no purpose to existence, there must be a God.

A rather circuitous and devious argument, isn't it? In recent years this proof has been gussied up to become known as "intelligent design." The argument is that there has to be intelligence behind creation, because a purpose requires a design to achieve that purpose; and a design requires a designer to design it. Obviously that designer is God. Without God the delicate balance of forces which make up our universe would have destroyed it before it could be born.

The beauty of the intelligent design argument is that it states the case clearly; the universe just happened, for no reason, simply all of a sudden there it was, or the other choice, it was created. The Intelligent design theory says it had to be created because the universe had to be incredibly fine-tuned to even exist, much less to permit the emergence of life. The possibility of this simply happening by chance is mathematically highly improbable.

But then, improbable is not impossible! The Teleological or "Intelligent Design" proof is merely another theory, and one which is not accepted by the majority of philosophers or scientists. Since it is not the number of votes that decides whether something is true, the argument continues to have many adherents.

The third argument: the Rational Proof

The point here is that it is simply rational to believe in God because the universe is completely obedient to natural laws. Einstein's general theory of relativity proved it is specifically obedient to the laws of mathematics. In fact, the universe is utterly, slavishly predictable in this obedience.

Why? Well, says this theory, because God set it up that way. That is the only rational answer because apart from an act of God everything would simply exist in chaos. But whether this argument is rational or not, it is still only an argument, or theory. It is not even close to being proof, and nowhere near being generally accepted in science or philosophy.

The fourth argument: the Moral Proof
This is another very reasonable argument which points out human beings not only have consciousness, but a conscience, a sense of right and wrong, a belief that some things are simply moral and right and some are immoral and wrong. This is universally true throughout history and in every culture. So, the argument claims, this proves there is a God behind the creation of the world because God has instilled this moral sense into human life.

That doesn't mean we will never do anything immoral or wrong, but we know even as we do them that they ARE wrong and immoral. On the other hand, mercy, truth, love and integrity are good things. We know this because it is an innate conviction which God placed within us.

I like it, but behaviorist psychologists would certainly disagree with the entirety of the reasoning. Of course behavioral psychologists are not the arbiters of what is true, so there we are....an intriguing argument, one many of us like, but still only a theory not a certainty.

The Fifth argument: Religious/Humanist Proof

This is my term, because I conflate two philosophical ruminations together in this final argument. It is my term but not my argument; I am only presenting it. The point of it is that the very idea of God would never enter human minds unless God put it there; therefore belief in God is an essential component of being human. This idea leads us with a very seductive hand directly into the argument that human history itself proves the reality of God in the very fact that humans believe in God and act on that belief.

I call this a seductive argument because it is so hard to disagree with it! It resonates deep within us and we feel it is true. After all, as far back as we can trace it; humans have had spiritual experiences, the transcendent, the numinous, the holy experiences seen in the earliest days of human life. Many of the Neanderthal cave paintings are almost supernatural in their overtones of spirituality and sensitivity.

We also know that early humans very carefully buried their dead in expectation of an afterlife. If there were not a sense within us that God exists none of this would have taken place. Therefore God exists! I will admit that for me this one is the most convincing of the bunch, even though it too falls short of being irrefutable proof.

Brief as this has been and compelling as we may or may not find these arguments, none of them are an expression of the Christian faith. We had to start with them because, as we move into what the Christian faith does say, remnants of these proofs or arguments are still hanging around.

Self-styled atheist Christopher Hitchens loved to quote the inadequacy of these "proofs" as indicating that Christianity is foolishness because they do not prove God exists. As much as I really enjoy his writings, Hitchens didn't seem to understand that Christianity is not in any way based upon those theories and is completely indifferent to all these philosophical efforts.

The huge difference between the Christian faith and these philosophical "proofs" is that the Christian faith does not argue the existence of God; it strongly affirms, rejoices and proclaims that God exists. It then adds defiantly that God knows and cares about each one of us in an ultimate and eternal manner.

This understanding comes only through faith as the Holy Spirit speaks to us. This assertion lifts the whole equation of God's existence out of the realm of speculation into personal affirmation.

To the Christian faith the existence of God is an existential reality in our lives. As the book of Genesis in the Hebrew Scriptures says: "In the beginning God." Then, along with the New Testament, adds "…in the ending God."

God is in the beginning and God is in the ending. Let us now proceed to fill in what the Christian Faith has to say about the middle part of those two assertions.

2

Does God Exist?

Those "proofs" we considered are far from compelling, and the question "Is there a God?" remains uncertain. It is certainly not obvious there is a God. We cannot see, smell, or touch God so how can we know?

In human history, when our senses fail us, we seek ways to improve upon them. When we couldn't see far enough to understand the universe around us, we invented the telescope. When we could not see the infinitesimal world we knew existed we invented the microscope. Unable to run fast enough or far enough we invented the train and the automobile, the boat and the airplane, moon rockets and Mars probes and all kinds of wonderful inventions. All these things increase our knowledge of the world we live in. But do they help answer the question of God's existence?

To ask, "Does God exist?" is actually to ask, "Why should God exist?" and ultimately science and philosophy have no acceptable answer to that question.

As we have seen in the previous chapter, philosophy has exhausted considerable effort trying to solve this problem. But in the end, all philosophy has been able to do is assemble a variety of arguments, some sophisticated, or apparently so, some not so much so, and some actually awful. However none are conclusive, and none constitute "proof" God exists in any honest sense of the word.

The same difficulty confronts us when we turn to science to prove the existence of God. Science primarily operates by the so-called empirical or trial and error method; that is, postulating a theory and then, by verifiable experimentation, proving or disproving the theory. But the question of whether God exists is not one that can be answered by experimentation.

It is equally true for the majority of the big theories of science in physics and cosmology, that there is very limited ability to verify by experimentation. Mostly they are "maybes." Some of these possibilities are better than others, some more reasonable than others; but all are only theories.

Unfortunately, without the validation of repeatable experimentation, they must remain merely theories, which exist uneasily within the discipline of science and more comfortably within the discipline of theology. This is because to believe a theory, or accept it, without objective proof and without repeatable validation requires faith in either the theory or in the theoretician behind it.

Don't be surprised by this for post-materialism science, known as quantum physics, has thrust all science into the same arena as religion, and wrapped it in the same dilemma that faces religion.

Without verifiable proof the fundamental assertion on which the theorem or postulate is based is ultimately one of faith. The theorist believes the theorem is right, but cannot prove it and thus can only have faith the theorem is true, and that the process of further investigation will either support the theorem or eliminate it.

So, in the end, those who say, "If God cannot be proven by reason (philosophy) or science, then God does not exist," seem not to realize what they are saying. There is no way to prove God exists. Yet, as the poet William Cowper is credited as saying, "...absence of proof is not proof of absence."

On the other hand, it is equally true absence of proof is not proof of presence either, so it is still possible

God does not exist. This leaves us with a circuitous dilemma. Does God exist? Does God not exist?

How can we determine an answer to this vexing question? And, even more important, how does God's existence or non-existence impact me? How does it matter in my daily life? This is more honestly the real reason for questioning or believing in God's existence; how does it matter to me? In the next chapter we will consider this extremely personal and yet very universal question.

3

The Existence of God is an Enigma

Because the question of God's existence can neither be proven nor disproven, it could be said to be like Winston Churchill's famous comment on Russia, it is "a riddle wrapped in a mystery inside an enigma." While one of the most oft quoted of Churchill's insightful aphorisms, the end of it is usually left out. Churchill ended by saying, "...but perhaps there is a key." Yes, a key there is to the question of God's existence, and it is the hope of this book to clarify that key.

Philosophy and science have sought the key with great diligence and hopeful expectation, but the results have been disappointing and the existence of God remains an enigma. If there is a key, where is it? The key cannot be discovered by either philosophy or science because they base everything upon reason and reason is not the key.

We owe so much to the so-called "Age of Reason," and/or "Enlightenment," which began with a bang in the 17th century and flourished in the 18th century, that it seems almost ungracious to be critical of it. However, in spite of the great achievements this age unleashed, criticism is nonetheless deserved.

The enlightenment era was driven by two main impulses; the certainty that the human mind could, by using reason, understand all things, and repugnance for religion bordering on outright hatred. The enlightenment era set about with malicious abandon to use the first reason to literally tear apart the second... religion. It attacked the Christian faith with such vitriolic passion that much of it continues to bear poisoned fruit in our time.

While, strictly speaking, outside the parameters used to define the Enlightenment era (roughly 1695-1815), the work of Sigmund Freud (1856-1939) is a good example of the corrosive residue of the Enlightenment.

Despite of the strong insights he brought to human self-understanding, we can largely blame him for planting the idea that God is merely an illusion left over from our youngest years, when we had an infantile need for a father figure. A need, he said, we have outgrown, because civilization had matured and no longer required a father figure and thus no longer needed God. In our maturity, reason (and psychoanalysis!) has taken the place of faith, and science the place of theology.

Poor Mr. Freud is largely discredited today, and some of his theories discarded as naïve; but nonetheless he left a legacy of anti-spirituality in the literature of psychology, which has spilled its toxic musings into fields completely unrelated to mental health, among them philosophy, science, and theology.

One of Dr. Freud's most famous contributions to psychology is that, when we are faced with a reality which for whatever reason we cannot bring ourselves to admit, we "repress "it.

Repression is a basic tenet of psychoanalysis and means we move what we cannot consciously admit from the conscious mind into the unconscious mind, where hopefully it will not continue to bother us. In other words, we deal with unpleasant or terrible things by not dealing with them, but by putting them in the basement and locking the door.

Unfortunately that does not end the matter for whatever is stored there, uncomfortable and unhappy, keeps attempting to come back to the main floor, to the conscious mind. It expresses this desire in dreams, anxieties, compulsions, and sometimes in inappropriate behavior.

Apparently Dr. Freud did not realize that this basic assumption, so foundational to psychoanalysis and modern psychology, that the unconscious mind largely governs our conscious behavior, applied to him as well as to his patients!

Nor apparently did he see that by his own theory, the persecution and prejudice he had to endure for being a Jew would likely have been repressed. In order to maintain his prominent social and medical position in society it could not be admitted. However, as his theory insists, what is repressed always bangs on that cellar door and requires of us a constant checking on the strength of the lock on that door.

This makes me wonder if perhaps it was the denial of prejudice and persecution against him, which was very real but which he could not admit, that led to his avowed atheism. If we apply to him his own insights, using his own terms, was he perhaps unconsciously angry or disappointed with God for not being the "father" he needed in that difficult time?

I have ventured into all of this because, while our concern is not psychoanalysis but theology, unconscious motives may be as much involved as conscious ones in affirming or denying the existence of God. For example, I may believe in God because my life is so blessed that a good God must be behind that. Or, conversely, I may believe there is no God because if God did exist, surely he would not be so indifferent to my wretched situation. Since God cares, God exists. Since God seems not to care, God does not exist.

It is said all politics are local. So also the question of God's existence is ultimately not a question of philosophical debate, or scientific uncertainty or even theological difficulty. It is local in the sense that it is personal. All belief in or denial of God is personal. We love God or hate God, believe in God or deny God, because of personal experience we have had with God. Or lack of it.

We do not generally go through the day applying philosophy or science or theology to the events of our lives. We just move through the days bouncing from one event to another, like a loose ball bounding down the street, just letting things happen. After all, as Cyndi Lauper said, "Girls Just Want to Have Fun." Of course boys do too.

Yet, when we think about what the existence or non-existence of God means for us, we immediately run into Churchill's enigma, a circular confusion of logic, theory and uncertainty. But I said there is a key. The key is Revelation. Without revelation, there is no answer. With revelation the door opens and the answer comes clear. We need to look at Revelation next.

4

Revelation is Absolutely Necessary

The dilemma of the human situation is that apart from revelation we simply cannot know what is true about God. Philosophy, psychology, every discipline has tried to prove the existence of God but in the end, as Descartes finally concluded, the only truth we can know is that "I am".

I am. Not "who" I am, not "why" I am, not "for what" I am, but simply that "I am." That's the best answer philosophy and sciences are able to give us.

The five requirements of journalistic reporting and police interrogation methodology, "Who, What, Why, When, Where", are thought to have been originated by Aristotle who said they are the questions we need to ask to get at truth.

While the Aristotle approach has been generally the method of understanding for more than 2000 years today we are not so sure. It is now maintained that for human beings truth is mutable, that is it varies, and depends on the situation, upon who is asking, and most of all …most of all …it depends upon "Why" we are asking.

The problem is that while "why' is the most important question of the five for contemporary thought, it is also a most unreliable witness. It depends upon interpretation and thus is susceptible to the vagaries of human emotion, experiences, fears and hopes. Human nature lies! So who can believe it?

Even so, we still want to know! We still need to know! It is absolutely necessary for us that we know "why?" It is the question we have asked from the dawn of human life, and still ask every day: Because if God exists then "why"…did this happen to me, why this illness …why did my son die? Why, and why now?

The question "why?" is endemic to being a human being and yet in our 21st century wisdom, it is denied relevance and importance because there is no meaningful answer to "why" apart from the existence of God.

And therein lies the problem, because the existence of God can only be known through revelation; and for the secular world revelation is simply not an acceptable proof or answer.

The problem quickly becomes more difficult if revelation is not an acceptable means by which to answer why things happen. It becomes "choose your poison," bad luck perhaps, a bad horoscope maybe, or possibly the sophisticated "chaos theory" in which the flap of a butterfly's wings can be the "why" that set off a hurricane.

Pick one of those or some other explanation, but whatever you choose, expect the unexpected, because that is almost certainly what will occur. That is how life is and there is nothing to be done about it. We need to be crystal clear here. The universe is so complicated and interrelated that if we put aside revelation as the means by which to understand it, then chance, luck, probability is the best we can do to comprehend why things happen.

And this is so even though chance and luck are poor answers, and probability contains within it the caveat that it may not be true or at best may be only possibly true. And even if it is true, it is still uncertain and subject to change.

Without revelation, some kind of guesswork is all we have. But current culture and society cannot abide the concept of revelation, so next we look at some of the secular alternatives to Christianity.

5

Creation in the Secular World

Since the secular world does not allow for revelation, 21st century cosmologists have determined to their satisfaction that as far as understanding the creation of the universe is concerned, it is not required! In his book "Grand Design" Stephen Hawking postulated that creation did not require a creator! The universe simply came into existence from nothing slightly less than 14 billion years ago. It all burst forth in a 'big bang" of energy release which created the cosmos.

Fortunately, we have the residue of that big bang to examine and from which to deduce our suppositions. Unfortunately, there is no way to know anything about what existed, if it existed, before the (supposed) "big bang" explosion that brought the universe into being.

Or ... maybe it was not a bang, but a bounce?

While the majority of cosmologists no longer doubt the Big Bang theory as the best explanation for the origin of the universe, until the late 20th century the

Big Bang theory was very much in doubt. The prevailing and majority view was what is called the "steady state universe," the view that the universe has always existed and always will.

Science lives within the uncertainty that is endemic to all human life, and in these first decades of the 21st century many cosmologists have become unsettled by the Big Bang theory. As new information is discovered, a myriad of changes and adjustments are required in order to hold it. So the old steady state idea is being revisited, but with quantum physics twists.

Some are now proposing that the Big Bang may really have been a "Big Bounce," that is, just a moment within a continually expanding then contracting steady state universe that has no beginning and no ending. Instead of bursting forth in a big bang, basing their hypothesis upon quantum mechanics and Einstein's theory of general relativity, more recent opinion suggests the Universe has simply been going on forever.

Thus, what was thought to be a theory settled fifty years ago has again been called into question. Science deals with what is probable but not conclusive and largely depends upon how you want to look at it. Big bang or steady state are both an option and you can take your pick. In other words there is no certainty; and new theories and ideas are brought forth almost every day.

However, there is near universal agreement that big bang or steady state, or big bounce, whichever is true, the earth itself, this planet on which we live, came into existence a bit less than 5 billion years ago. How that took place is not clear, but it is agreed the earth in some manner was formed out of the dust and debris that was present in the universe. The how is not known, and the why is even murkier because we only know what we know.

Former Secretary of State Donald Rumsfeld referred to "known knowns," things we know we know, and "known unknowns," things we know we do not know. He also said there are "unknown unknowns," things we don't know we don't know. Secretary Rumsfeld was speaking of the difficulty of making military assessment, but it certainly applies to cosmological speculation, a field in which in which unknown unknowns abound!

One huge example of that is what has been termed "Dark Matter" or "Dark Energy." We know both dark matter and dark energy exist because their effect upon the universe can be measured. We do not know for sure, but those measurements have led to the probability that about 68% of the universe is dark energy, around 27% dark matter, and the remaining 5% is called "normal matter."

Normal matter comprises everything we know, all we have ever studied and measured in the universe or on earth. All we can see and all we know are in that 5% which we might call the 'known knowns." All the rest, 95%, is in the category of things we do not know.

The humbling fact is 95% of the universe is a complete mystery and "why" remains mysterious as ever. Science has no answer, and it remains elusive because it is really a religious question. A question for which the Christian faith does have an answer, and we move to that answer next.

6

Creation in the Christian Faith

Christianity says the total commitment of God to human history is seen in the incredible statement that "In the beginning God created the heavens and the earth." (Genesis 1:1) This affirmation the Christian Faith shares with our Jewish brethren and in principle with Islam as well.

But there is a difference. The Christian faith asserts that the "why" of God's creative activity, that difficult and often elusive three letter word, is intrinsically and completely tied to Jesus Christ. In that assertion Christianity stands alone. The bold claim that Jesus Christ pre-existed his incarnation on earth and was/is a participant in the act of Creation sets the Christian faith apart from all other religious understanding. Neither the Jewish faith, Islam, nor any other religion would easily agree with the involvement of Jesus Christ in creation.

The Gospel of John puts it this way: *"In the beginning was the Word and the Word was with God and the Word was God. He was in the beginning with*

God and all things came into being through him, and without him not one thing came into being." (1:1-3)

St. Paul echoes that in his letter to the Colossians: *"He (Christ) is the image of the invisible God, the firstborn of all creation; for in him all things in heaven and on earth were created, things visible and invisible, whether thrones or dominions or rulers or powers—all things have been created through him and for him. He himself is before all things, and in him all things hold together."* (1:15-18)

Then in his letter to the Romans Paul again says: *"From him (Christ) and through him and to him are all things."* (Rom.11:36) This is a difficult concept because it does not intend to say God determines everything that takes place, but to say that everything that does take place, whatever the immediate cause or source of it, ultimately it is subject to God's will.

The ambiguities of life however are so profound, the evidence so confusing, that for all of us there are moments when we simply don't know what we believe. And whatever we choose to believe there is no absolute assurance it is correct.

While what we want to believe is that God's hand is behind everything that happens in our lives, we can never know that for sure. It might be God's will at work, it might be the devil, it might just be bad luck. It might be genetics, our own fault, or the sin of the world.

And even when it seems that our prayers are answered, that might be God at work, but it might be good luck, good doctors, or good genes for healing.
There is no way to be certain. That is, no way to be certain apart from revelation! No way without the personal experience of the Holy Spirit. Minus that assurance everything about God is ambiguous. God's presence in the world, in our lives, none of it can be proven.

This is a bit of a dilemma, isn't it? And it would leave us completely adrift and without hope were it not that God WANTS us to find him. God reaches out to us by coming among us in his incarnation in Jesus and by sending the Holy Spirit into the world to seek us out and bring us to him.

I love a poem by Francis Thompson titled the "Hound of Heaven." Poetry is always the reader's interpretation, and mine is that Thompson depicts the Holy Spirit as a bloodhound who stays on our trail, hounding us through life, barking, nipping, and nudging us until finally we stop running away, stoop down, pet him, and find God.

All of our own efforts to "find" God only end in confusion and uncertainty. But all the while God is seeking us, pursuing us until we stop and let him find us. And when we stoop down, when we open the door, the Spirit rushes in, and it is for us as it was for St. Paul...the scales fall from our eyes, that dark and distorting mirror in which we see life comes into focus, and suddenly we see the truth that was there all the time.

It is the assertion of the Christian Faith that we are not here because the elemental stew of the big bang explosion was precisely right and out popped life. No, we are here because in the void that was nothing God whispered those incredible words: "Let there be light," and there was light and day and earth and stars and creation and all that is.

Now all of this would simply be another theory, except for revelation! Except that a soft but clear voice whispers in our ear, "Before you were in the womb I knew you, and I chose you to be my child." (Jeremiah 1:5) That's why I did all this, God says, all for you...and for all my sons and daughters whom I love with an everlasting love.

The Christian Faith says that in whatever happens, in all that happens, God stands with us, and nothing can separate us from God's presence and love. This is God's world. And God is very much in control of it.

7

The Origin of Life on Earth

Whichever theory you like most (big bang, big bounce, or steady state) as best cosmology knows right now the universe came into being about 14 billion years ago, and those who study such things tell us the earth was born approximately nine billion years later; five billion years ago. Those are only estimates but it's good enough for me.

However, exactly when in the process of the earth being formed, life came into being on earth, and how life came into being, and even more important why life came into being is still a mystery.

What is less mysterious is how life developed after that moment when it came into existence. The process by which life developed from that initial moment is a theory termed "evolution." Now we need to be clear that for all its widespread adoption evolution is only a theory, one explanation of how things could have developed, from the first simple life forms into complicated human beings.

Evolution is not to be taken as absolute fact, though based upon the evidence we currently have, it seems to biology and other scientific disciplines that evolution is the best way in which to explain the means by which human life developed.

Science remains non-committal on the question of whether that development was directed by God or by chance and has no appreciable information to contribute to the question of why life exists at all.

The thing is, what gives the theory of evolution high marks, is that so far it is the best way to group and understand the vast amount of information we have about life; human, animal, plant, bacteria, etc. In other words it is a theory that works very well. But it is possible that it may be superseded someday by a better or fuller understanding.

Whether that happens or not, the Christian faith neither embraces nor denies evolution as the origin and development of human life. The "how" of creation is interesting, but not of ultimate importance; that distinction belongs to the question of "why," the ultimate question of the Christian Faith

The reason the theory of evolution may someday be replaced is that, to whatever degree it is accurate and correct, it has only a partial and uncertain understanding of how the first self-replicating life forms developed from what they were into the next more advanced stage. Understanding that final step is crucial, but to science it still remains an "unknown unknown."

While the Christian faith would say that God is in control of the universe, and is involved in the whole process of creation and development, it would also admit that the means or manner in which this all took place is indeed a mystery.

Still, something in us always wants to solve mysteries, and it is tempting to seek traces of God's hands here and there in the evolutionary process. So some point to the fact that all life comes from one common source shared by all life on earth; all human DNA is 99.9% the same for everyone. And the most recent evidence is compelling that all human life descended from one pair of ancestors!

Many would also point out that the earth was formed out of dust, and the Bible says, "Dust thou art and to dust thou shall return." (Genesis 3:19) But as much fun those commonalities between current science and biblical writings are, the fact remains the Christian faith is all about "why" God created, not "how" it was done. The "how" is, to be sure, important, but "why" is fundamental to everything.

Unfortunately, from the secular viewpoint there is no answer to "why." Secularism merely says regardless of how it happened, we are here, living in a world of sometimes chaos, sometimes order, often good often evil, with no explanation or reason why this is so.

Philosophy too has long debated and theorized but ultimately while it offers a variety of possible explanations, none of them ring solid or true.

****

Into this void of certainty, the Christian Faith asserts that however creation precisely took place, and to whatever extent chance and probability may have been involved in the process leading to human beings, God did not leave it to those means alone.

The Hebrew Scriptures are vibrant testimony to the fact that at the beginning God did not simply set creation in motion and then sit back and watch what happened next. To the contrary, God has been an active participant in the unfolding history of the world. The important word here is "history." When creation began history began and God was there.

The Christian faith joins Judaism in this, and equally maintains that God was in the beginning and has ever since remained active and very involved in human history. While to be sure God's very involvement in creation has, by necessity, left fingerprints in nature, tantalizing hints and touches of his presence here and there. This is not in any way conclusive evidence of God's participation in the creation process and those "hints' are very ambiguous.

It is only as we look to human history with what Christianity calls "the eyes of faith," that we can see God has been completely "'hands on" throughout everything. Isaiah, that most incredible prophet, reminds us of this in Isaiah 45, which I slightly paraphrase: "The Lord took Cyrus (Cyrus the Great, ruler of Persia (600 – 530 BC) by the hand…. saying although you do not know me, I know you and I have anointed you for my purposes. Therefore, I will go before you and level the mountains, I will break in pieces the doors of bronze and cut through the bars of iron, I will give you the treasures of darkness and riches hidden in secret places so that you may know that it is I, the Lord, the God of Israel, who call you by your name."

Cyrus is only one of many examples of God's hand at work in human history. Recounting them is beyond the intention of this book, but all of them are only a prelude to God's total commitment which takes place as God becomes incarnate in Jesus Christ. That is the heart and soul of the Christian faith and of this book.

8

The Church

St. John's on the corner or St. Timothy down the street are the visible signs of the reality that is "the Church."

That reality is shrinking, and except for the continent of Africa, church membership has been in decline for the past decades. Europe was the vanguard of this tendency, preceding the United States by at least two generations.

Some would speculate the decline in church attendance in Europe was the result of two great wars, which devastated everything, and the horrors and inhumanity of both Nazism and Communism which so quickly followed.

Surely true, but in addition it is impossible to even calculate the extent to which problems within the Roman Catholic Church have impacted that exodus. The sexual predation of priests, the perceived misogamy of the curia, the continued second-class citizenship of women, and the unwillingness of the church to accept changing sexual mores of society, are perhaps equally a part of the decline of religious interest.

For many believers, "Where was God in all this?" became the question. And bereft of an answer to that question, existentialism, atheism, secularism, communism and a potpourri of other ism's spread across the countries. Today it continues to flourish in the widespread attitude of "who cares," which holds current society in its grasp. And for many the churches and the Christian Faith have both become irrelevant.

What God wills is no longer a question of interest to the world, and what God says, no longer a viable answer to anything. The opinion of the German philosopher, Friedrich Nietzsche, that "God is dead" is the new Mantra.

Of course Nietzsche meant his phrase in the sense that Pascal had meant it centuries earlier; that God as a viable philosophical concept was dead. Nevertheless Nietzsche's words have come to mean that God as any kind of reality is dead and there is no God. If once there was a God that God died and is no more.

And then it follows naturally that if there is no God there is no need for the church. No need to go to church. And even if, by some extremely remote chance there is a God, (because who can know for sure?) still there is no longer any need for the institutional church, because anyone can reach out to God by being "spiritual."

While it is not a new idea, this assertion that we can meet God "spiritually" has become the model of the day. The collectivism of communism has been replaced by the individualism of secularism which insists that religion as such is dead and gone, and if a person is nonetheless inclined to faith, then all that is needed is personal spirituality, not the institutional church.

Well, once again yes, that is true, but no, that is not true. It is true that this is what is taking place, but it is not true that what is taking place is correct understanding.

From the very first believers who gathered in shared amazement at the resurrection of Jesus, the church has known itself to be a community brought together by faith in Christ Jesus. The church has long used the term "fellowship "to express the relationship that believers have with God, through Jesus, and with each other in his name.

In 1st Corinthians 1:9, Paul states this clearly; *"You were called into the fellowship of his Son, Jesus Christ our Lord."* Paul both indicates the relationship believers share with Christ and each other, and the fact that it is not by our choice or doing that we are in this fellowship but that we have been "called" into it.

From the very beginning, the "Church" understood itself to be a fellowship of believers in which the Word was proclaimed and understood by the guidance of the Holy Spirit who was vigorously at work within it to develop and strengthen its faith.

This is exactly the *view of the apostle John, who wrote, (1 John 1:3) "That which we have seen and heard we proclaim also to you, so that you too may have fellowship with us [that you may share in what we have seen and heard]; and indeed our fellowship is with the Father and with his Son Jesus Christ."*

The story of the church as it moved from its early beginnings into the world is a fascinating tale told in many places by many authors, some believers and some not. As we might expect, the perspective from which the author writes determines to a large degree the conclusions which relate that history.

But even the most ardent supporter of the church would agree the history of the institutional church is checkered, with false starts and dead ends, beautiful achievement and disastrous alliances.
No matter which history of the church one reads, it is clear the church is not perfect. Indeed, by its own admission it is a collection of sinners. This is perhaps no better seen than in the fragmentation of the church which began almost as soon as the fellowship came into existence.

It became clear early that not all believers understood "The Faith" in the same way. Differences ranged from mere nuance to near abrogation. Battles, wars, splits and recriminations plagued the fellowship and continue to do so, an unhappy truth we cannot deny. Nor can we pretend differences of theology did not occur or that they do not remain in the church still today. To pretend that deep divisions are not still present within the body of Christ would be foolish in the extreme.

From the very beginning of the community, division and difference of understanding existed. After Paul had established the church in Galatia and moved on in his missionary effort, others followed him with a strongly different view than what Paul had taught them. Paul sarcastically called them "super apostles" who, of course, knew better than anyone else what the faith was all about!

In similar manner Paul noted that he had to berate Peter to his face over Peter's effort to play both sides of the fence in the community's uncertainty about the necessity of keeping kosher rules. (Galatians 2:11)

Less controversial, and more common in the fellowship was Paul's remonstration to the Corinthians that, while some could only tolerate mush (a surface understanding of the faith), in actuality the gospel was red meat! (Difficult, highly nuanced, and requiring tolerance of differences).

Paul said, *"And, I, brethren, was not able to speak to you as to those who are spiritual, but as to those who are carnal - even as to babes in Christ. I gave you milk to drink, and not meat; for you were not yet able to receive spiritual meat; and neither are you able now, for you are still carnal. For since envy and contention and divisions are among you, are you not carnal?"* (1Corinthians 3:1– 3)

No church or denomination has a monopoly on the true understanding of the Faith. None of us has as yet arrived at that point of certainty. The Danish philosopher Soren Kierkegaard said that no one is a

Christian; we are all in the process of becoming a Christian. And Augustine said if anyone says they understand God it is not God they understand.

But it would serve no good purpose to attempt to relate the theological differences in the various denominations of the church. They exist, they are important. And they are not at all important.

They are important because they continue to divide the fellowship and cause unfortunate disagreements, and sometimes bitter words and accusations. Not surprising since the church is a gathering of sinners!

But they are also not at all important because the church is not only a collection of sinners; it is equally a collection of saints. And the most essential and definitive characteristic of the church is that we are all one, *"We all confess one Lord, one faith, one baptism, one God and Father of us all, who is above all through all and in all."* (Ephesians 4:5)

Still, it is true not only of theology, but science and philosophy as well, that differences of understanding lead to differences of opinion. Since this can cause confusion, the faith is expressed in "doctrines" and "dogmas" which try to clarify what the church believes. We look next at some of those doctrines and dogmas which tell us what the church has said about some of the difficult questions of life and death.

In the end, though, the church is merely an earthen vessel in which the word of God, the grace and forgiveness of God are held, for the purpose of being shared, preached, and taught. The highest treasure of the church is its ministry of Word and Sacrament, the "means of grace" by which believers are nourished in our faith. That comes next.

9

Baptism

Baptism is a particular, definite, unrepeatable action of the church through which we are called out of created life as we know it into an intimate relationship with our Creator. We who are born of dust and doomed to return to dust, become, by a gracious act of love, sons and daughters of one who in our baptism is no longer merely a cosmic power, but our heavenly father.

For most of the history of the world a child came into the world through intercourse between a man and a woman who then became the child's "Father" and "Mother." That is still true for the majority of births; however in current society other methods are also employed. Intrauterine Insemination (IUI) inserts semen directly into a womb. While a sperm donor, a male, is still required, it need not be the woman's husband, she need not be married, and the child may be raised by a two female or two male families.

In another method, "in vitro fertilization" (IVF), a woman's eggs are harvested, fertilized by sperm in a lab, and then the resulting embryo implanted in a uterus. It can be any woman's uterus, and the whole process may use eggs, sperm or embryos from anonymous donors, and the uterus used may be that of a surrogate.

In this new world of such biologic muddle and its resulting gender confusion, we are lesbian, gay, bisexual, transgender, or questioning. Thank God for baptism, which reminds us that whatever the process through which we were born, whatever the human family unit in which we live, God is still our creator. And whichever gender with which we associate, or the process through which we came alive, everyone born into this world will die.

We don't have to live very long in this world before we see the ocean of pain and suffering in which the human race is trying to swim. The longer we live, the more people we see who seem to be drowning in a sea of misery. With sadness and sorrow we soon come to realize that in so many ways we contribute to that misery, occasionally with purposeful intention, but most often simply by neglect or default.

We may not mean to do it, intend to do it, but we contribute to each other's pain and suffering by what we say, by what we do not say that we should say, by what we do and do not do. We are guilty people, and there is no way we can be free of our guilt, unless someone takes it away from us.

In baptism that is exactly what happens; our guilt and sin are washed away in the water of baptism. This was much more dramatic when the person was immersed completely into the water and lifted out again. While some churches still baptize in this manner, most simply sprinkle water on a person's head. Both are valid because the method is merely the outward dramatization of what is happening.

In a much more essential way, the water of baptism represents life in the most basic way possible. Without water there could be no human life. We float in a watery substance almost from the moment of conception, and we cannot live free of water from that moment on. We need water to live. And we need the water of Baptism to live the new life, the forgiven, redeemed life in Jesus Christ.

In the Christian Faith baptism is the means through which we are brought into the family of God and made brother or sister to the Lord Jesus Christ. Baptism underscores the eternal meaning and purpose to the lives of each one of us. In times of pain and sorrow we can turn to God and we don't have to say "Almighty Power;" we can say "Father,"

"Mother" and God will respond, "Yes, Wayne... Yes, Mary..."

In our baptism God addresses us by name, and from then on whenever God speaks to us he says "It is you I am talking to." Our name is important, and for each one of us in our baptism it becomes the definition of who we are. As St. John says, *"What love the Father has given us, that we should be called the children of God. And that is what we are."* (I John 3:1)

While some Christian communities prefer to postpone the sacrament of Baptism until the person being baptized is able to make the event his or her personal declaration of faith, there is a fair amount of disagreement about this within the Christian community.

For all Christians baptism is an act of God in which we are "adopted" into the family of God, so in that sense it does not matter at what age we present ourselves for baptism. However, in the majority of churches the preference is for infants to be baptized. There are at least two good reasons for this:

1. Coming to baptism as a child with no accomplishments with which to impress God

heightens the truth that God chooses us, we do not choose God.

2. When baptized as a child, he or she can grow into a personal understanding that all the benefits mentioned above were given to them by a gracious God who loves them and embraces them as a loving father or mother and will forever treasure them as his or her child.

While infant baptism may be the preferred method, baptism can be given at any age there is no prerequisite of age or circumstance.

Is baptism necessary to be saved?

The short answer is, "No."

Baptism is not necessary for salvation.

The whole thrust of the gospel is that the love of God is boundless, limitless and without condition. Therefore, the imposition of Baptism as a prerequisite for God's love or for salvation is anathema to the very nature of God. It is not lack of baptism that is problematic to salvation but rather disdain for it, or the assumption,
"I do not need it."

If we refuse to come closer to God, our refusal drives us further from him. In the final sense, while Baptism is not absolutely necessary, why would we withhold it from anyone if it is within our power to give the joy of knowing you have been redeemed and are loved by God?

It is a wonderful thing to be able to say, as Martin Luther said so often in times of distress and confusion," I have been baptized …I am a child of a loving God." Baptism is the person's incorporation into the family of God, and the lifetime benefits of knowing you are a child of God are immeasurable.

10

The Holy Spirit

The book of Acts recounts the events which took place at the "Council at Jerusalem." The principal reason for the council was to deal with the controversy created by "certain individuals who came down from Judea insisting circumcision was necessary for salvation." This created great consternation among the Gentile members of the church for whom circumcision was not a heritage issue. (Acts 15)

Peter made an eloquent speech saying, *"God, who knows the human heart, testified to them (the Gentiles, the uncircumcised) by giving them the Holy Spirit, just as he did to us..."* (Acts 15:8) Paul who was also at that council added testimony of how the Spirit had worked within the Gentile communities with which he was familiar.

After deliberation it was decided by the Council that Judas and Silas would be sent to Judea to correct that erroneous circumcision requirement. They made this decision on the basis that "*It seemed good to the Holy Spirit and to us...*" (Acts 15:28)

This little encounter and the decision which followed illustrates how the early church understood the Spirit to be present among them, leading and clarifying the young and growing church.

Of course this was not a new discovery for the church. The Spirit had been equally at work among and within the Israelite communities. The book of Genesis reports that in the beginning, at creation, "a wind from God swept over the face of the waters." (1:2) The Hebrew word "Ruah" (wind) was used for the invisible presence of God, the Spirit, working God's will not only in the creation, but also in the history of God's people.

"Spirit" in both the Hebrew Scriptures and the New Testament, is the word for the power or presence of God moving among us. As Elijah said, the Spirt may come among us in a rushing wind of sound or in a small quiet voice, but when the Spirit comes it is understood to be the presence of God.

The early Christian community understood that presence to be with them to bring clarification of Jesus' words and to give guidance for faithful living.

Jesus identified the Spirit as a "wind which blows where it wills....you hear its sound, but you cannot tell where it comes from or where it is going. So it is with everyone born of the Spirit." (John3:8) It was left to Paul to take that further and begin a serious theology of the Holy Spirit.

Paul was convinced that Jesus' resurrection also resulted in his ascension and took him directly into the presence of God. Therefore, in Paul's view, from that moment on the Spirit is intimately identified with Jesus.

Arguably this understanding is true for Mark and Matthew and John as well. They agree that having been raised from the dead, Jesus immediately ascended to God the Father. (The Gospel of Luke is an outlier in this and is the only gospel to record that Jesus ascended 40 days after his resurrection.)

The intention of the gospel authors was to make it clear that the Sprit cannot be thought of as a vague, formless, disembodied power blowing about the world. Rather, in the same way that Jesus is the incarnation of God in human life and history, so also the spirit is the presence of Jesus in the community of faith.

Those who talk about not needing the church because they can be "spiritual" would only receive from Paul a large helping of scorn. He would say, "You can't have one without the other." Because, while the Spirit is indeed blowing through the world, the task and purpose of the Spirit is, as Martin Luther put it, to "call, gather, enlighten and preserve us in the true faith of the church." The spirit leads us to Christ who is present in the Word and Sacraments and fellowship of the church.

The presence of the Spirit is the presence of God with us, and the Spirit is bound to the Church in the same way God has bound himself to Christ. It is the presence of the Spirit in the community which calls us to faith, fills the water of our baptism with God's presence, and brings us into the family of faith called the Church.

The presence of the Spirit does not cease with our baptism but remains with us, continues to enwrap our lives with its presence, inspires us to love, leads us to do justice, and strengthens us in faith.

11

Holy Communion...
The Lord's Supper

While Holy Communion is the most sacred sacrament in the Christian faith, there is strong disagreement in how it is understood. Each denomination has its own way of doing this.

Roman Catholic and Eastern Orthodox Churches:

The Roman Catholic Church understands that in the act of consecration, performed only by a validly ordained priest, the elements of bread and wine are changed into the body and blood of Christ.

This process is termed "transubstantiation," and the change from bread and wine into body and blood of Christ takes place to such a complete degree, that any wine remaining after the consecration must be drunk by the priest and/or deacon. It cannot be simply disposed of because it is no longer wine but the blood of Christ.

Since wine is essential in the Lord's Supper, the priest attempts to consecrate only as much wine as needed for the celebrants because non-clergy communicants generally receive only the bread not the wine. (This is changing in less conservative parishes.)

The reason for limiting the distribution of the wine (blood) is a practical one. The Catholic Encyclopedia assures communicants that in the bread alone Jesus is fully present with his entire body and blood, the entire divine presence. Therefore, since the bread alone is efficacious for salvation, wine is not necessary.

The decision is also driven by the practical matter that it is difficult to give the cup to perhaps hundreds of people without spilling at least a small amount of the blood of Christ, which, for the more conservative in the church, would be a grievous problem.

In situations of ecumenical concern, at a wedding, or perhaps a smaller gathering of worshippers, both elements may be received. Basically it is concern for practical matters that determines whether both elements of the sacrament are administered.

Orthodox, Lutheran, Anglican, Reformed, and Methodist churches:

In strong distinction to transubstantiation, in these churches the words of consecration have no power to transform the elements and the bread remains bread and the wine remains wine. It is believed however "in, with, and under" these two elements, Christ is truly present among the community in the sharing of the bread and wine.

Basically, the main thrust of Holy Communion for the entire Christian community is to remember and celebrate that in His death and resurrection Jesus achieved the forgiveness of sin for all.

As the congregation remembers that night of the supper, it celebrates the fact that our sins have been forgiven in the sacrificial death of Jesus in our stead.

As we take the bread and wine into our hands we are spiritually joined with the Lord who is present among us in the worshipping community. Thus Holy Communion is the celebration of what Christ has done for us. And as we celebrate Jesus joins us. As a community we remember, as Jesus bid us do, that in Him is our forgiveness.

Other Protestants:

Many Christians are able to accept transubstantiation of the bread and wine into the body and blood; others only agree that Christ is truly present in the communion. Still other Christians are not able to accept either transubstantiation or the real presence of Christ in the sacrament; they prefer to understand that the bread and wine are symbolic of the mystical presence of the Body and Blood in the Sacrament.

And yet, while there are different understandings, ultimately the differences are somewhat inconsequential, because for all the Christian denominations, Holy Communion is the very life's blood of the community of faith which we call the Church. It is Jesus' consummate gift to all believers that we can take his very presence into our hands. Whether we understand that to be physical presence or spiritual presence, for all Christians Jesus is with us as we celebrate communion, personally present for each of us.

The deep personal and incredible reality is that the body and blood of Christ were "given and shed for you." Those are the words that matter. Those are the words we need to hear. "Given for you... Shed for you." Those words change everything. The meaning of the bread and wine is that Christ gave his body and shed his blood so that we might live.

But it is not merely the body of Christ that we share, we also share the fellowship of the church. That fellowship is, in a true and deep sense, also the "body of Christ." We take into our hands the body and blood of all those who have held us, and loved us, and taught us, and cared for us.

It is the body of our mother, our father...tired and worn from labor in our behalf...that is broken for us. It is the life's blood, shed for us in all those hours spent to care for us. It is the body given for us in all the anxiety, the fearfulness and sleepless worry that was gladly given for our sake.

The Lord is there, present in all of that, his love reaching into our lives through those who love us. Christ is present among us, present within us, present for us, as we gather in his name, and that's what we share in Holy Communion as we take the very life and love of God into our hands.

It is no wonder the church has different views, because how can that be put into a doctrine? How do we explain all the love, the forgiveness, the sacrifice, the tenderness that God has given to us over the years in those who have loved and cared for us?

The presence of Christ comes to us in all those who have loved us and who continue to love us. All of that swirls in the cup, and while we only receive a tiny taste, it is enough to make us remember and give thanks for so many...who were...who are....to us...the body of Christ.

I understand Jesus to have included all of that when he said, "Do this to remember…"

12
Hell

"What the hell....?" "The hell you say." "I feel like I've been through hell."

What do those expressions mean? When we say them, what do we mean...what are we saying? Do we believe in hell? Why do we believe that? Why don't we believe it?

In the Bible the concept of Hell is complex and dynamic. In the Hebrew Scriptures the word generally used for hell is Sheol, the general meaning of which is "the place of the Dead." Jesus used both the term Hades and Sheol in four parables (Matt:11, Luke:10, Matt:16, and Luke:16).

He also referred to the Valley of Hinnon, or its other name Gehenna, a large depression area outside Jerusalem. Running south and west alongside the city, it was actually the town garbage dump; and just as today in many such dumps a fire was constantly burning. Hence it led to the "fire of hell," "burning in hell," etc.

Perhaps based upon the image of that garbage dump (and the idea that only garbage goes to hell?), over the years hell was developed into a place of eternal fire and punishment for evildoers and/or unbelievers. The New Testament makes seven references to hell as a place of fire and punishment. For those who care to look it up: Matthew 5:29, 13:40-42, 25:41; Mark 9:43-48: Revelation 20:10, 20:15, and 19:20.

In early theology, as the church was developing, the church leaders, Origen and then Augustine, held that God intended no one for hell, and only those who deliberately chose to do so would go there.

Initially that understanding included Saint Augustine. Then later he completely reversed himself and concluded that because of original sin everyone must be destined for hell unless God chose to save them from it. Augustine was a powerful voice, and imprinting this grim opinion upon the church, he influenced the theology of hell for centuries to come.

Even in the church today his view is not only widespread but also the most popular understanding of hell. That is, hell is your destiny unless....you live right ...or believe right ...or ?

However, Augustine's view is very unfortunate, and Origen and the early Augustine are far more in line with the faith of the church. Hell is less a literal place than it is a term for the worst, most terrible, horrible situation we can image.

Jesus said we assign people to hell again and again, not only verbally but by how we abuse them, demean and dehumanize them by our actions towards them in this life. He said hell is what we do to people. And hell is what we do to ourselves.

It is not so much a place, or a time; hell is beyond both place and time, beyond longitude or latitude, years or centuries. Hell does not so much have a physical location as it is the experience of abandonment and loneliness, those "hellish" times when we feel we are, or really are, forsaken of human love and touch.

The families of slaughtered students in school shootings were thrown into that hell …and there is at least a degree to which we do that to each other again and again. To be in hell is to be bereft of God, or to feel we are bereft of God, bereft of love, outside the concern of anyone.

To be in hell is to be wherever God is not. It is a description of the reality that to be without God is to be dead in the most literally real and complete way possible. If we are not in God we are in the place of the dead. There is no longer any life within us. As Jesus said, "God is a God of the living not the dead." (Luke 20:38)

It is generally thought outside the church, that to be in hell is to be beyond the love and concern of even God. It is to be forever dead.

No question, there are times and situations when we feel we are without God, without even the possibility that God knows or cares about us. When we are in the absolute depth of human loss, everything is overwhelmed by the certainty there is no hope. To feel we are beyond even the concept of hope, to feel the world has ended, life has died, and meaninglessness has wrapped itself around us so completely there is nothing of value left in living, what truly can we call that except being in hell?

When there is no hope, when there is no possibility of redemption or relief, when there is nothing but the certainty that there is nothing; that, in its unrelenting torment, is what the Christian Faith means by Hell.

And yet, although it may be confusing, when we say in the Apostles Creed that Christ descended into hell (or to the dead), it intends to tell us there is no situation beyond redemption, no place beyond the love and concern of God!

The love and grace of God continues to be offered to us unceasingly until we refuse to accept it. God's love for all humankind is unconditional. There are none that are beyond God's offer of redemption and forgiveness. And that love of God for all creation is the answer to the question that arises in every generation; "What about those who died before Jesus, or those who in their life did not know of Jesus," etc.

Well, God sent his Son Jesus into human life and history, and being God, he is not bound by any restrictions. God is not limited only to events during Jesus' lifetime, nor is God limited geographically. This is God's world, history is God's realm, and whether dead or alive we are and remain God's creatures.

As quantum physics is telling us, every moment of time contains every moment of time. Past, present, and future are not mutually exclusive of each other but exist together within every moment. To me this is a way of saying there is no time when God is not there. Nothing…time, distance, life or death… is beyond the reach of God's power.

And yet, also, I do not intend to eliminate or deny the actual existence of hell. In some sense there is, must be, a hell, for God's love can be refused. And if refused, then hell becomes a metaphor for the dead who choose not to live. Then hell is truly the place of those who, whether dead or still alive, for whatever reason, will not accept the life that God offers them.

And if we choose not to live in God, who is life, then we are not living, which means we are dead. Not being in God we are in hell, wherever it may be.

13

Who Will Go to Hell?

The biggest problem with the popular misunderstanding of hell is that we see it as punishment for sins. This is an unfortunate confusion which came into the church gradually over its long medieval history. But it is a total misconception. Hell is not punishment for sins

As St. John says (John 3:17), "Indeed, God did not send his Son into the world to condemn the world, but in order that the world might be saved through him." God's intention for all his children is that they live in a relationship of love with him and with each other.

The story of Adam and Eve in Genesis is a metaphoric way in which to show us that we are all created with the whisper of God still ringing in our ears,"…you are my child, I love you." But as the story continues, it shows us the desire to live free, without the constraint of God's will, is powerfully within us as well.

Our problem is that, because of the power of sin to distort truth, we do not understand freedom, and mistake it for being able to do our "own thing." We reach out for the forbidden fruit precisely because it is forbidden, and because "no one is going to tell me what to do!"

The result is the existential reality we all know: guilt, brokenness, hurt, a relationship destroyed or put into great peril. When we do what we want to do because we are determined to do our "own thing," when we seek to live only for ourselves, when we seek nothing but our own will, we soon become slaves to our desires.

It is an escalating situation in which an act of self-will gives birth to another act of self-will and soon becomes a power that consumes us. As Paul puts it, when we sin we become a slave to sin, and soon we are a captive to it and no longer free to not sin. Once we have committed a sin it is so easy to do it again, and again, until it is just what we do. And we become sinners!

The Gospel of Mark shows us powerfully how this happens. Mark says that every time we do not accept the grace of God which comes to us in so many ways... acts of kindness, forgiveness, understanding; every time we rebuff them, push aside grace and forgiveness, our heart becomes hardened.

Oh, only a little hard at first, not yet solidified, but the hardening is a cumulative process. Hard-hearted Hannah's heart gets harder every time she refuses grace or love. Every time she chooses selfishness or greed instead of love, her heart becomes just a little harder. Whenever she refuses God's will and demands that her own will prevail, her heart hardens a little bit more. (The feminine gender here is of course inclusive of both genders!)

The end result is that finally her (his, our) heart is hard as a rock and no longer has any interest in love or forgiveness, we become unable to even think of anything but our own will and desire. Eventually a stone-hard heart can no longer beat, and we literally die to real, honest, or meaningful life. We run from it because a heart of cement cannot hold it.

So, only those who choose to be there will be in hell. Jesus said, "God is a God of the living not the dead." (Luke 20:38) This was said as an affirmation of God's power to raise us from the dead, but the obverse is equally true. There can come a time when, by our own choice and refusal, we put ourselves beyond the power of God to save us. Then we are in hell and we have chosen to be there. Simply put, to be in hell is to be dead to God and to stay dead to God. God will not resurrect those who persist in demanding their own will prevail. Jesus said to refuse grace and forgiveness when it is offered is the only unforgiveable sin. And if sin is unforgiven it reaps its due. (Mark 3:28-29) Even psychology shows us the inevitable truth of this.

Hell is the other side of heaven. Possibly a literal place....but, most of all, a way of saying that dying is inevitable, but arriving at the fulfillment God desires for human life is not inevitable. It is possible to get lost along the road and never arrive at the intended destination and instead to wind up in hell.

In recent times the World Council of Churches determined that the phrase "descended to hell" should be changed to read "descended to the dead." Both are equally accurate, but I don't like "descended to the dead," because it destroys the juxtaposition with heaven; and in my opinion, if we change the first half of the phrase, we should change the second half as well.

That is: "He descended to the dead, and on the third day he ascended to the living." To do that however would really muddy things up because it needs to remain clear that Jesus' resurrection was ascension to God…ascension to heaven… not merely a return to living again.

But the real reason for the change, as much as anything, is that the Council of Churches, in agreement with the majority of more contemporary sentiment, does not like the term "Hell." They dislike it because the whole popular understanding of hell as a place of everlasting torment, fires and punishment, is so spread through popular culture, it gives a mistaken understanding of both God's grace and of forgiveness.

Ok, I get that, but I still don't like it. Personally, I will continue to say, "He descended to hell and he ascended to heaven."

Heaven comes next …the other side of Hell. But before we get to heaven let us consider the question of what some have said is a middle ground between hell and heaven: "Purgatory."

14

Purgatory

I include this brief excursion into a strange and complicated idea because it seems so sweetly reasonable on the surface that one is inclined to nod acceptingly.

Purgatory is about a second chance, and should not everyone be given a second chance? And would not God who is love beyond bounds be inclined to give that second chance? And if so, should there not be a way for God to provide a second chance? Yes, we say, there should be. Well purgatory is that second chance. There is no basis in the New Testament for the concept of purgatory, but it was developed by the church because of its apparent reasonableness.

Reasonable it is, but it does not work without the companion idea called the "Treasury of Merit." This equally reasonable idea was developed in the 13th and 14th centuries. It was needed because in complete distinction to what the early church had taught, the medieval church understood salvation to be dependent upon how well we lived our life in this world, how many good deeds or how many bad deeds we committed.

Once this qualification for salvation had been established, that good deeds were required to be saved, an obvious problem arose; how many good deeds were needed to go to heaven? And how many bad deeds or lack of good deeds will send us to hell?

Well, they said, that number is something only God knows. Yes, but it seemed to common sense and reason, that there must be a minimum amount of good works a person must achieve in life in order to qualify for heaven.

And it would only be fair that whatever that minimum number, if you achieved it, you could enter heaven. Even though it might be by the skin of your teeth! On the other hand, if you did not achieve this minimum standard of goodness, it was only fair that you could not enter heaven.

The next development in the theory was the obvious necessity that accounts had to be kept of those good deeds. It must be shown to God that the minimum had indeed been achieved. But what if you fell short by only the slimmest of margin? Would it be fair to send some to hell who had achieved 99.9 % of the minimum requirement? No, that didn't seem right.

Fairness and rightness thus required the next step in this ingenious problem solving. That step was something called "The Treasury of Merit." This was based upon the assumption that those who are truly faithful will achieve not only the minimum needed to enter heaven (whatever the minimum is) but their good deeds will add up to somewhat more than is actually needed. God would surely not want this extra merit to be wasted, so it would be placed into a "treasury" maintained by the Church.

Solely by its own discretion, the church could draw out merit from the overachievers and apply it to those who did not quite reach the minimum, thus enabling them to enter heaven.

The beauty of this is that the treasury will never be exhausted because it contains not only the good works of the faithful but of all the righteous… the good works and extra merit achieved by Christ, the Virgin Mary, and the saints. The treasury is overflowing with good works to be utilized as needed.

In case you think I am concocting this incredible but lovely idea; it was put firmly into Catholic doctrine by Pope Clement VI in 1343.

The Catechism of the Catholic Church states it this way: "This treasury includes all the prayers and good works of the Blessed Virgin Mary. They are truly immense, unfathomable, and even pristine in their value before God. In the Treasury, too, are the prayers and good works of all the Saints, and all those who have followed in the footsteps of Christ the Lord and by his grace have made their lives holy and carried out the mission in the unity of the Mystical Body."

The good news was the amount of merit at the church's disposal is unlimited. The bad news was this whole idea was subject to abuse. It was a nice idea… a treasury of merit from which the church can withdraw, bestow upon sinners, and make them adequately holy for heaven.

It was a good idea but an idea ripe for abuse. And it was flagrantly abused in the 1500's by a Dominican prior and inquisitor, Johannes Tetzel. He sold indulgences with a used car salesman's enthusiasm.

The manner in which Tetzel sold indulgences was so extreme one could purchase one to free relatives from purgatory. His well know tweet was: "As soon as a coin in the coffer rings, the soul from purgatory springs."

After the Reformation the Catholic Church denounced the abuses of the Treasury of Merit, but was not willing to go as far as Martin Luther sarcastically suggested: that out of love the church simply give everyone enough merit from the treasury to get into heaven!

No, that was a bridge too far, and the existence of the treasury remains church doctrine. The sale of indulgences continues as well, because, as the Roman Catholic Catechism states," they provide a way to reduce the amount of punishment one has to undergo for sins and to encourage the performance of works that redound, not alone to the welfare of the individual, but also to God's glory and to the service of the neighbor."

So, with the treasury of merit firmly in place, purgatory was a natural next step. It provides a place for those who have not quite achieved the necessary level of righteousness to enter heaven, but who are good people. In purgatory they can experience a level of punishment which will purify them and make them eligible for heaven. A slimmer and modified version of purgatory is also present in the Greek Orthodox Church as well.

It is to Dante Alighieri's poem "The Divine Comedy" (Written between 1308 and his death in 1321) that we owe the popularization of purgatory. Still, it remains Roman Catholic doctrine in 2021.

Another aspect of purgatory is the idea of "limbo," an effort by the church in the Middle Ages to wrestle with the problem of unbaptized infants when they die. As babies they never had a chance to earn merit so it does not seem fair they should go to purgatory. What to do?

Easy, do the Limbo!

The Roman Catholic Church defines Limbo as "a state which includes the souls of infants who die subject to original sin and without baptism, and who, therefore, neither merit the beatific vision [heaven], nor yet are subjected to any punishment, because they are not guilty of any personal sin."

While this was a compassionate effort to work around a difficulty created by the doctrine of purgatory, it was never satisfactory, and in 2007 with the blessing of Pope Benedict XVI, the Catholic Church ended Limbo.

Purgatory, with new and mystic nuances, is still an official doctrine of the Roman Catholic Church, and has widely entered into popular thinking.

After purgatory, if it does exist, comes heaven so we turn to the question of heaven next.

15

Heaven

My, oh my, what confusion exists about the concept of "Heaven!"

Over the years heaven has pretty much been understood as a place where we hope to go when we die. Then, in recent years we have been deluged with dozens of books written by various people who had a "life after death" experience, in which they went to "heaven." The difficulty with those stories is that you have to be dead to get to heaven and if you are dead, you don't come back to tell of it. If you do come back to tell of it, then you were not dead!

Now that doesn't mean those people who claim they went to heaven did not have a spiritual experience. I think most likely it was a spiritual experience they had because the majority of them say they "came back" resolved to live a better life and that they understand grace and forgiveness in a way they never had before. So, a spiritual experience of God, yes, but truly an experience of heaven in the sense of the Christian Faith? Well, maybe, or maybe not.

The whole question of what happens after death has become enwrapped in philosophical and popular mythologies: ghosts, apparitions, zombies, and other diaphanous beings which fill the popular imagination. Mostly we laugh at these concoctions, and yet they continue to beguile us with thoughts of "is it possible?"

Well, for Christians life ends in death, then resurrection to new life. But when does this happen? Exactly when are we resurrected? And what will that new life be like?

Jesus was resurrected immediately after death, and St. Paul says our resurrection will be like his. So, when a loved one dies, we properly say to each other he or she is in heaven. This is the view of the New Testament; when we die, we are with the Lord.

And yet the body still lies in the grave, or the ashes remain. This led many in the church to semi-adopt the view of Socrates, Plato, Aristotle and the Greek philosophers. They speculated about a soul, or spiritual aspect to our being, which is released at the time of death and goes to heaven, leaving the body behind. This idea of an eternal soul is a very popular conception. But what would eternal life be without a body?

Here we have to deal with the problem that, over the centuries, well-intentioned but erroneous efforts to clarify what happens in death, and after death, have muddied the whole question by confusing it with those Greek philosophers. The result has been an understanding of heaven which allows, almost promotes, "life after life" experiences. This Plato view understands death as escape from the troubles of life in this world, into a "heaven" of glory, angels and total spiritual well-being.

But that is not the Gospel….that is not any of the four gospels. I don't want to hasten the coming chapters on the end of the world and eternal life, but the New Testament says nothing about souls fleeing physical life for existence in some kind of disembodied spiritual heaven.

Actually, popular though it may be, this philosophical contemplation is erroneous, subversive, and treacherous! In the Christian faith the "soul" does not leave the body behind as it soars its way to heaven. To say it does misrepresents the faith's entire understanding of what death is and what resurrection means.

The New Testament understanding of resurrection is, as the Apostles Creed states it, "I believe in the resurrection of the body." Not a "soul" or ethereal spiritual entity. When writing to the church in Rome Paul told them: "the one who raised Christ from the dead will also give life to your mortal bodies through his Spirit who dwells in you." (Rom 8:11)

Paul insists it is this body in which we live that will be given life again. But he also terms this resurrected body a "spiritual body." (1Cor 15:44–46) by which he means our physical body will be given spiritual qualities in resurrection. This will make of it a new and imperishable body. In the theology of St. Paul, it is emphatically the entire person, that is resurrected, not merely a "soul."

When the resurrected Jesus appears to the disciples in the gospels, it was in his body, or at least in the form of a body. My book, "Then is Now," has a fuller development of this; but in summary, the gospel accounts are highly stylized theological accounts, not intended to be understood as a literal visitation of Jesus… in the same body he had before death.

No, the resurrected Jesus did not have the same body he had in his life on earth. And the gospels describe his resurrected body, as being able to go through a locked door, as in the upper room gathering, (John 20) or to disappear suddenly as it did in the Emmaus story. (Luke 24)

Paul says in the same manner that will be true for us. In our resurrected life we will inhabit an imperishable body not like the perishable body we now inhabit. The "perishable," he says, "cannot inherit the imperishable..." (1 Cor. 15: 50)

For us this raises the question whether we will recognize each other. Will I know my husband, will my wife know me? Neither the Bible, nor the Church, deal with this question directly so there is nothing specific that can be quoted as an answer to the question. However, indirectly and by inference, the answer is "yes," but not necessarily in the way we may think, because it will be an imperishable body, not the same perishable body in which we died.

Jesus says that the power of God will change us to be like the angels, neither marrying nor giving in marriage, but becoming a new creation. (Matthew 22: 30) And Revelation 21:4 says, in heaven "there will be no death, no crying no weeping, no more a babe ripped from its mother's arms, or an old man walking around in confusion." In other words, resurrected life is not like life on earth.

What it will be, in my opinion, is described for us in

1st Corinthians 13 where Paul says that "...while now we see in a mirror, dimly, then we will see face to face. And though now we know only in part; then we will know fully, even as we have been fully known. Faith, hope, and love abide," he says, "and the greatest of these is love."

That will be life in heaven. The greatest thing is love, and our love for each other will continue. It will still be there, but it will no longer be a perishable love. It will be imperishable, eternal, purified and wondrously real. We will love as God loves, perfected and holy and without blemish: love that understands and accepts and forgives and lives forever.

That is a theological description of heaven, but it's the best that we have in answer to what life will be like in what is for us a mysterious and unknown realm of existence.

The Christian faith does not answer everything, but then we do not have to understand everything. Actually we cannot understand everything anyhow. That is true perhaps especially in regard to heaven, and may be why Jesus said about the details of heaven, "Only God knows." (Matthew 24:36)

But even if we cannot know all the details, we need

to know who will go there! Will I go to heaven? Will my beloved be there? Who will go to heaven?

The Christian Faith answers "everyone who wants to." And be clear, don't get it wrong, in Christian theology God's salvation is available to all people in every race, every culture, every religion, geography, and time. We are all children of God and all are embraced by God's love. None will be excluded from heaven.

Except.......

This is simultaneously the easiest and hardest thing to understand; that all will be embraced by God's love except those who want to be excluded. John's Gospel says that some love the "darkness" (his metaphor for life without God) and will prefer the darkness without God to the light which is life with God. In that case they will not be in heaven where God is; they will be in hell where God is not. But it will be their own choice, by their own will and desire, that they will be in hell and not in heaven.

But, but, but we say ...if all who want to be saved are saved, then what about judgement? Are there not some things that cry out for judgement! Must not God "payback" the atrocities of ISIS, Hitler? Are not some things so vile they are beyond forgiveness? Yes, to be sure that would be so if I were doing the judging. But God does the judging ...Jesus does the judging ...and while we are not privy to what that judgement will be, we do know that God has, for Jesus' sake, determined that forgiveness and mercy will be offered without end to all who will accept it.

Now before you cry "foul," realize that Hitler and all the truly evil in the world will not accept mercy and forgiveness even if it is offered to them on, as we say, "a silver platter." They have embraced evil so completely, their hearts have become so hardened, they will laugh at the very idea of mercy and love. They will not want it and will spit upon the offer. For the rest of us, sinners in varying degrees, but sinners all, the Christian Faith asserts that for Jesus' sake God forgives us.

I want to address this more fully in the chapter on Atonement, but in the end, in the whole matter of sin, hell, heaven and forgiveness, we must live with mystery and clouded understanding. It is as the prophet Isaiah put it: "For my thoughts are not your thoughts, nor are your ways my ways, says the Lord. For as the heavens are higher than the earth, so are my ways higher than your ways and my thoughts higher than your thoughts." (Isaiah 55: 8-9)

That is not a put down of humanity; but a realization of the prophet that we are the creatures not the creator, and some things are simply above our pay grade.

This leads us to the next chapter in which we deal with what resurrected life means for those who do choose to live in the light, those who do accept the forgiveness offered by God's grace and, in that acceptance, enter heaven and eternal life.

16

Eternal Life

If there is one aspect of the Christian faith that we all eagerly embrace with hope it is the promise of eternal life. It is the last sentence in the Creed, "I believe in life everlasting," but it is of first concern in our lives. Who would not want to live forever?

But if what we are promised is a continuation of what we have, if to live forever is to live life as we know it, but without end, would we really want that? Would that not become boring? We get bored from time to time in this life as it is, and to think of those occasions going on forever; that's more like a horror story.

However, that is not what is meant by "eternal life." When a loved one dies we say they will always be remembered … but even as we say it, we know that it is not true. They will be forgotten. Oh, they will remain in our hearts for as long as we have consciousness, and maybe they will remain beyond that as a name in genealogy to be discovered by some great, great, great, descendant, but essentially life forgets us all.

To the world, to reason, to history as we think of it, we simply do not matter. In Christian Theology the doctrine of eternal life is a way of saying "not so fast." We may not matter to the world but we do matter to God. God will remember us and will see to it we are not forgotten.

The promise of eternal life is the promise that God who is the creator of life, who in Jesus has redeemed life, will bring all things to good and proper ending and then to a new beginning. This God who embraced us in Baptism and has forgiven us in Christ Jesus, this God who loves us, will see to it that when our life ends we will not end.

In the Christian faith eternal life is all about you and me, each of us as individuals, as children of God who are known so personally, the very hairs of our head are numbered.

And those hairs will remain in our new eternal life …metaphorically speaking! That is, not exactly in a physical sense, but in the most essential sense, eternal life will be a spiritual continuation of the very human life we are living right now. It will be "me" who is resurrected: my consciousness, all that I am.

Perhaps the best way to understand how this can be is that the Christian faith asserts we are living within eternal life at this very moment. It is not only a future gift we will be given, but it is also a gift of the Spirit right now.

Paul says that when we are in Christ and when Christ is in us, we are no longer living in our own life and by our own power, but we are living in Christ and by his power. And the Gospel of John (5:24) says: "Whoever hears my word, and believes him that sent me, has eternal life, and comes not into judgment, but has passed out of death into life."

Ok, this is confusing and questions continue to abound. For example, what about those whose bodies have been lost at sea, or burned in fires? For many years various denominations of the church opposed cremation because it destroyed the body and if it was destroyed, how could it be resurrected?

I guess it was thought burial was better than cremation because at least the bones were still there to be raised again! (The ankle bone connected to the leg bone…)

St. Paul cut through all the foolishness and speculation when he gave an extended answer that I recommend you read in 1st Corinthians 15:35-50. But in summary Paul says "flesh and blood cannot inherit the kingdom of God, nor does the perishable inherit the imperishable." That is, it is not our physical body that will be resurrected, but a "spiritual body." It will be the person, our self, our personality, that which is us and makes us who we are, that will be resurrected. The body will be new but the person inhabiting the body will be remarkably the same person we are now.

Understood this way, the resurrection of the body is another way of saying that to be living in Christ means to be living a resurrected life right now. We will be the same, and those we love will remain the same, and in that new life they will be there with us and everything that was good and beautiful will continue to be good and beautiful.

And yet everything will change, for those dark and sour days, those fearful and conflicting days, will be gone. Those limitations, the fears and sins, the inadequacies we live with now will be no more. The Alzheimer's that has plagued our loved ones will be no more and they will sparkle as they once did. That is the promise of eternal life.

But do not ignore that central assertion of the Christian faith we made above, that in the most essential sense, eternal life is not only a future gift, but we are living in eternal life every day right now. And therefore every day we are living in the loving hand of God. And just as Jesus lived in intimate relationship with God, so also do we. God is our Father and Jesus Christ our Savior.

Right now, in this day, we are part of the family of God with all the rights and privileges that entails. WOW!

It might be best to think of eternal life in terms of the quantum realm in which we currently understand ourselves to exist. It is a world of unlimited potential in which any imaginable outcome is possible.

In the quantum world, time is not something that flows from past to present, but rather in every moment of what we experience as "now," the past present and future are all mixed in together. All are there in the present moment even though we are not aware of it being so.

Except that sometimes we are. Those déjà vu experiences of having been here before, or having experienced something before, and precognition experiences in which we are aware of something about to happen which has not yet happened. Those are perhaps insights or even examples of living in God's time.

Albert Schweitzer put it this way, "I am in Christ; in him I know myself as a being who is raised above the sensuous, sinful and transient world, and I already belong to the transcendent. In him I am assured of resurrection; in him I am a child of God." (A. Schweitzer, The Mysticism of the Apostle Paul (ET London, 1953) pg.16.)

So eternal life, life in heaven, will not be a static repetition of what is now but a continuous adventure of what is yet to be as we live in the wondrous grace and unfolding newness that is God. It is true even in heaven that the best is yet to come! How exciting!

17

Sin ... Original Sin ... Evil

One of the biggest confusions in the Christian faith is how to understand the fact of Sin. From personal experience we all know that sin is a reality...but why? And where did it come from?

When the faith of the church was still in process of development it was vulnerable to the influence of many philosophical and theological ideas, some current to that particular time, some centuries old even then, some that remain with us still.

As the early community of faith moved into the Greek-Roman world it was necessary to have a firm position from which to battle with the philosophical arguments and attacks of that world view. In the give and take of this necessity, what was to become the "orthodox" faith developed. For reasons that are beyond the scope of this book, orthodoxy adopted a literal approach to interpreting Scripture, both the Hebrew Scriptures and the New Testament.

Orthodoxy took the beautiful metaphor of Adam and Eve and redid it, actually twisted it, into an historical account of two actual persons who sinned by disobeying a direct order of God. Then the orthodox position decided the sin of Adam and Eve was transmitted by them through sexual intercourse to every human born thereafter. In that scenario Sin comes to each of us as a consequence of birth, so the term "original sin."

While the story of Adam and Eve's disobedience, called the "fall from grace," is a good story that has provided the plot for many books and movies, the true situation is a much deeper version of that.

The story of Adam and Eve is not about two historical people from a far distant time, but it is a description of you and me, and all human life. The "fall from grace" is a metaphor, a symbol, which describes the situation of every human being. We are Adam and Eve, and just as they do in the story, we disobey God because we prefer our own will to God's will.

And yet it is even deeper than that.

In the Genesis story Satan appears in the guise of a serpent to tempt Adam and Eve. It is of course again a metaphor, but metaphors are often best at capturing the deepest truth, and in this story we recognize ourselves. Each person knows that "sin" is a conscious act of will. We commit sins and we know it is sin when we do it. And it results in guilt, which is the child of our sin, bearing too much family resemblance to ever deny it is ours.

But the Christian faith insists sin, even "our sin," is not merely a private matter of a transgression having taken place between us and God. The entire human race is infected with Sin with a capital "S."

Your sin and my sin are brother and sister to each other...we are all in this together. We have all been possessed by a power of evil that is stronger than we are, and there is no escape from its clutches. We know from life experience that there is a power that exists, something more than, and other than, the impulses of our own minds, something dark and twisted, that seeks to grab us and consume us.

The Christian faith affirms the existence of this power. A power so evil, so conniving and sinister, it can only be called demonic. Satan is the name, the metaphor, for the fact that evil not only exists, but is personal to each of us as it tempts and seduces us.

In that way it is for us exactly as the Adam and Eve story captures so well; it is a seduction. But a seduction which, as it was for them, no one can withstand. We all succumb and hence we all suffer the consequences.

Some say sin is an act of a free will, something we choose to do. That certainly is accurate as far as it goes, but it doesn't go far enough to explain why everyone makes that same "free will" decision to sin! There is no one who does not sin. If sin is a choice, why everyone without exception chooses to sin would indeed be a mystery.

But mystery always brings with it the delusion that maybe we can solve it. After all we are pretty smart! And so we continue to endure, through all the efforts that have taken place down through the generations, to solve the mystery of why there is Sin. I say we must "endure" the efforts because the majority of those efforts have led us down a warped and sinister road to dark and dead-end alleys.

Determinism is one of the big dead ends. In this view whether or not we are a sinner is determined apart from any action on our part. It has been predetermined who will sin and who will be a saint. The game is rigged and all we can do is walk through our days until the prearranged end.

Those who are less religious, more philosophically or scientifically rigorous in their thinking, may attribute that pre-determination not to God but to fate, chance, or perhaps our genes.

But fate, genes or whatever the means by which it originates, determinism is a popular explanation because it suits our pride so well. If the reason we commit personal sins is because it has been determined for us, then it takes from us all personal responsibility. If God did it, or if we inherited genetic predispositions, it cannot be our fault!

But there is a price to pay for this guiltlessness; if there is no freedom of will, if we are all just dancing to the tune played by God or our ancestors, fate, or bad luck, we lose everything that makes us a unique person. In fact we are not a person at all, we are a puppet.

Vociferously in opposition to determinism, the Christian faith asserts that Sin with a capital S exists independent of the sinner. It is a power present in creation which seeks every opportunity to exploit our weaknesses, and we are unable to resist. Even though every one of us believes we can have a dalliance with sin and give it up anytime we want to, like the alcoholic who deludes himself that he can handle "just one drink," it is a fallacy.

In truth we cannot. Once Sin comes through the door, it is too snaky, sneaky, devious for us. We cannot stand up to it, and soon we become an indentured servant, what St. Paul calls being a slave to Sin. (See Romans 6)

This bondage is a status from which we cannot break free by ourselves and from which we must be redeemed by a power greater than our own. That redemption is offered to us freely, in Christ Jesus.

The confusion with determinism comes in the fact that if we refuse to allow the power of God to redeem us, then that refusal does indeed determine our future. But that future is one we have entered into by our own choice, not by a quirk of nature or plan of God. We are slaves to sin but it is because we have sold ourselves for one reason or another.

Another dead end is the popular theory that sin is not a weakness or a choice but rather an aspect of our evolutionary heritage. Those animal instincts and impulses, still latent within us, the so-called law of nature which we cannot overcome, leads us to deeds which are natural for the animal we are. This, the theory says, can only be called sin by ignoring the fact that we are only acting as a child of nature.

There is attraction in this for many, who note that just as we cannot expect a lion not to prey on wallabies, we cannot expect a human not to obey the natural impulses within us to prey upon each other. Therefore, we are bound to be promiscuous, or possessive, or any other action which we can term "only being human."

It is a fascinating theory, but it does not adequately explain the rest of human drives and emotions; the will to power, the will to dominate, the desire to subjugate. Nor does it explain the selfishness and hubris, the cunning, subterfuge and calculating self-interest that is shot through the whole human condition.

Sin is a power existing not so much intrinsic to creation as in opposition to it. God did not create it and it exists contrary to God's will. The Christian faith does not attempt to explain this but affirms that the origin of Sin and Evil is a mystery.

All we know for sure is that it exists. We see it clearly in our unwavering disobedience to the will of God, our disregard for what is "right," what is "'just," what is "moral." To sin is to ignore all of these whenever, for our own reasons, it suits us to do so.

Still, while the origin of sin is unknown, it is a fact of life, a bitter and undeniable fact that seems to come with every breath we take. And to be caught "in Sin" is a very serious matter not to be lightly dismissed. It cannot be pushed aside or ignored for it permeates everything and distorts the life of everyone.

Sin is choosing our will over God's will, and the result is we deserve God's punishment, just as Adam and Eve in the Genesis story deserved their punishment. Disobedient children must be punished.

That means the best we can hope for would be that the punishment fit the crime. But that is a frightful idea! Still, that would be our future, except that God has a different understanding of punishment and has done something to overcome it.

18

Atonement

"The Atonement" is God's solution to sin. The word atonement means to "make one again," that is, to restore our relationship with God that sin has broken, and to make it what God wills it to be.

In the years after what is called the "Apostolic Period," the first 100 years C.E., the church struggled to understand why Jesus had to die. Remember that the disciples and followers of our Lord were completely demolished and distraught at his death. Then suddenly they were elated and excited at his resurrection. But why did all this have to happen?

As the church struggled to understand why God required Jesus' death, four main explanations came out of that effort. They have been termed "Theories of the Atonement." While all four were inadequate from the beginning, they are nonetheless the best efforts of human reason to explain why Jesus had to die.

Unfortunately, but perhaps necessarily, to some degree each of them, or parts of them, have been incorporated into the theology of the church. They are inadequate efforts which have only added confusion and distortion to what God has achieved in the death and resurrection of the Lord Christ. But since they have been and are so popular in the church, they are worth considering.

The Satisfaction or Substitution Theory

The earliest of these efforts to understand Jesus' death came out of Jewish sacrificial practice. For generations on the Day of Atonement the Paschal lamb was sacrificed for the sins of the people. It was believed God would accept that sacrifice and grant forgiveness.

Therefore it was reasonable for the early Christian community to understand Jesus as a sacrifice to God in our place. While, because of our sin we deserve God's sentence of death, Jesus takes our place, substitutes himself for us, and dies in our stead. God accepts Jesus' death as ours and forgives us.

In other words, Jesus suffered as a surrogate for all humankind, thus satisfying the demands of God's honor in the face of human sin. This is not exactly the best Christian theology, but it has been a popular way to understand why Jesus had to die. We have all heard it in sermon after sermon. It has a tinge of truth and a dose of reasonableness, which made it one of the earliest ways in which the church came to understand why Jesus had to die. Many still prefer the Substitution theory.

The Christus Victor Theory

This is another early effort to understand the reason for Jesus' death. The idea is that he entered into the battle against the powers of evil...Satan and his demons. They killed him; but in his death he defeated the power they held over life and creation because in his resurrection he was victorious.

This is the view of the earliest Gospel, Mark, which tells us Jesus stood up against Satan and was rewarded by God with his resurrection. Then, in his ascension, Jesus took his place at the right hand of God, a reward which he won in his victory. He was the victor; therefore God gave him the power to rule and judge as King in the new kingdom.

While quite lacking, this view was arguably the most popular in the church for almost 1000 years. It fit well into the cultural system of both the early years of the church and the medieval times, when armies were either victorious or defeated; and to the victor went the spoils.

No matter that it was popular and congruent with the culture of the era, times change, and as the Middle Ages wore on this view lost its popularity to what came to be termed the Moral Theory.

The Moral Theory

Rather than the Gospel of Mark, this argument builds on the Gospel of Luke, whose main contribution to understanding the death of Jesus is that Jesus was innocent of all the charges levied against him. Luke states that those accusations against Jesus were trumped up by the religious leaders, and had no basis in truth. However, Jesus went along with it willingly to show us how we are to respond when acts of violence and evil are done to us. Turn the other cheek, give up your coat, love your neighbor, etc.

While always present to some degree around the edges of the faith from the beginning, the moral theory came to full development in the 12th century in the writings of the French abbot Peter Abelard (1079 - 1142).

Abelard said that Jesus died to show us how much God loves us, and to move us to emulate Jesus' death by loving each other no matter the cost. This theory continues today but perhaps with less fervor than before.

The Ransom Theory

This is the big one that still resonates in much of the church. It suggests that in their sin against the will of God, Adam and Eve sold themselves, and by extension all humanity, into captivity to the Devil. They fell from grace, had to leave the Garden and live with the consequences of having broken their relationship with God.

All humankind, as descendants of Adam and Eve, now also live in that broken state of existence and, like them, having forsaken God, are doomed to "living in sin" forevermore. But, God, wanting to restore the relationship, paid the Devil a ransom to free us. He gave the life of his only Son.

The Devil gladly accepted Christ's death as ransom and considered himself to have made a great deal. He thought that he had won. But what the devil didn't know was that God had an ace-in-the-hole. He didn't tell Satan he would raise Jesus from the dead and make him victorious after all.

These four theories of the atonement are among the early efforts of the church to understand the need for Jesus' death.

You don't have to pick one, you don't have to pick any of them; the church over the centuries has moved from one to another and then back again and often mixed two or more together. We have heard them all or parts of them in sermons and Bible studies.

But none of them are really satisfactory, none of them are really the Christian faith, and all of them leave us with questions.

The main and critical concern remains unanswered, because what becomes confused in the exposition of these theories is the intention, present in all four of them, to say that in Jesus' death we are reconciled with God.

That is the good news in all four theories, but it is unfortunately mostly overshined by the details and speculations of the theory. Still, the point, the intention in them all, is to say that the Sin in which human life and the world is held in bondage has been defeated and forgiven; and our relationship with God has been restored in Jesus. That's the point of all four theories.

Unfortunately, although interesting, they fall far short of really explaining what takes place in the death and resurrection of Jesus. To say that Jesus took my place, or that he possessed a power I do not and was therefore victorious in the battle against sin, or that his death is an example for how to live my life, or even that God so loves me he paid a great price to redeem me…are all true. But it's also true they distort, actually cheapen, what is really taking place in that incredible act of Jesus.

Ah…but you and I know we are not worth it! "Jesus died for my sins? But I am not that significant, and my sins are not worth the price he paid." And even if we add, as is sometimes done, that Jesus died for the sins of all people, the objection remains…the death of God's son is still overpayment.

We feel deep within us that if that's the deal then the devil did get the best of the bargain. But all that changes when we realize that Jesus died to bring an end not only to the power of sin in my life, and in all human life, but to totally destroy the power that Sin, Death and Evil hold over the world.

It is not overpayment if we realize that Jesus died to bring about the Kingdom of God, the reign of God in which Sin is no more. That kingdom so vividly described by the writer of the book of Revelation (Rev.21):

"And I saw a new heaven and a new earth: for the first heaven and the first earth were passed away; and there was no more sea. And I John saw the holy city, New Jerusalem, coming down from God out of heaven, prepared as a bride adorned for her husband. And I heard a great voice out of heaven saying, Behold, the tabernacle of God is with men, and he will dwell with them, and they shall be his people, and God himself shall be with them, and be their God. And God shall wipe away all tears from their eyes; and there shall be no more death, neither sorrow, nor crying, neither shall there be any more pain: for the former things are passed away. And he that sat upon the throne said, Behold, I make all things new."

Only when it is clear that the death of Jesus is cosmic in purpose and meaning can we return to the understanding that Jesus died "for me." Only when we put the big picture first can the personal one come into true focus. And we need to do this, and should do this, because the personal is what is of ultimate concern to us. In the end faith is personal. It is all personal.

All politics are local, and all theology is local, and Sin, Evil, even Death remain abstract concepts for every one of us until we can see how it involves us personally. And the atonement absolutely involves us personally, for if we do not enter the fight with Jesus against those powers that assail us, if we do all we can to simply sit upon the fence and not get involved, well then, we are uninvolved.

And if we are uninvolved then we are also un-included in what Jesus accomplished. Jesus often spoke about our need to "pick up our cross" and follow him. Not just follow him, but follow him as he carries his cross, carrying our own cross behind him.

It is only when we understand the atonement on a personal basis that we realize faith is not a passive situation in which Jesus has done it all and we simply stand there and receive the benefits.

No, no, it is through our participation in Jesus' fight against Sin that we are saved. We must join in the fight as combatants. Our participation does not earn us our salvation or in any way entitle us to it. Christ has achieved that for us, and through him God grants salvation freely to all who ask. But without our participation we are not involved in what Jesus has done; and if we are uninvolved then we are un-included in what he accomplished.

If that is confusing, that's ok. If this whole chapter is confusing, that's ok too. In the end we cannot understand the atonement and the whole mystery of why Jesus had to die. Let it be a mystery, just realize that as St. John assures us in words so simple, yet so profound, and oh, so incredible: *"For God so loved the world that he gave his only Son, so that everyone who believes in him may not perish but may have eternal life. Indeed, God did not send the Son into the world to condemn the world, but in order that the world might be saved through him."* (John 3:16, 17)

19

The End of the World

The theological term for the end of the world is eschatology. But whatever the term we use, nothing has so captured the imagination of the world as the end of it.

After the First World War T.S. Elliot wrote "The Hollow Men" in which he suggested the world would end "not in a bang but a whimper." That war produced such horror; such a loss of moral compass had enwrapped the world, that for all thinking people a total loss of hope had settled over everything. Lost and fearful, the world cried out in an empty groan of despair.

Empires had collapsed, long-lived countries were abolished, disillusion and despair held an entire generation in an iron fist. It had been, it was, too much to even talk about it. "Whimper" was the most apt word to describe it.

But then, after the Second World War, and the atomic bomb, that world view reversed itself; the world would end not in a whimper but in a bang. But whether in a bang or a whimper the fact that the world will end is a reality which has inspired poets, philosophers, theologians, scientists and physicists to weigh in on the manner in which the end will take place.

As we near 2021, amidst escalating conflict and terrorism, with rogue nations developing nuclear capabilities, we fear it might end in a bang of destruction as we explode a series of hydrogen bombs.

This is not an impossible scenario given the human propensity to absurdity, and the hubris which could end in the folly of nuclear "mutual destruction" envisioned way back in the 1980's.

That could happen of course. But even if it doesn't, it will; the sun is actually a gigantic hydrogen bomb. Somewhere about five billion years or so from now the Sun will run out of hydrogen, the solar system will come to an end, and it will all be sucked into one of John Wheeler's "black holes".

Or it could end with an asteroid collision as is said to have killed the dinosaurs. Science fiction writers suggest it could happen in a revolt of the artificial intelligence robots we are playing around with actually coming into existence and then rising up against us.

But perhaps it will end in a whimper after all; as the planet warms, climate changes and the selfishness and ignorance of politicians and world leaders simply ignore the danger which faces future generations. Even more imminent, the biological experimentation going on with plants, animals, and human DNA could spin out of hand and wipe us out as we experiment our way to extinction. As I write the Coronavirus threatens to do just that.

But one question exists in the heart of every doomsday scenario; if life ends, what has it meant? What is the meaning of life if it all ends, whether in a bang or a whimper?

Of course the same question is there in the ending of every individual person's life. Thus we could say death is the handmaiden of despair. But that has a sexist tinge to it which begs for a different image. Perhaps death is the henchman of despair? No, not much better!

But however we say it, death and despair walk through life hand in hand all the way to the bitter end.

Death leads to despair. Despair steals away any meaning from both life and death, and even the deepest of human relationships, even love, comes to naught in the despair of death. It ends relationships, ends everything that once mattered most. Death is the end of everything.

"Rage, rage against the dying of the light," said Dylan Thomas. Rage against it is about all we can do, for as everyone knows death is a natural biological fact of life. There is nothing to be done about it. And since life ends in death, and therefore there is ultimately no meaning to it, we are led to the conclusion of the writer of Ecclesiastes: "Vanity of vanities, all is vanity."

Or maybe not...

No, all the above is merely the conclusion of a world so caught in the grip of Sin and Evil it cannot comprehend the reality that the loving heart of God also exists in that very same fabric of creation and human history. God was there in the beginning and will be there in the ending. God is with us and has never left us.

But the secular world cannot accept that, and for those lacking the understanding of faith, the fashionable point of view is to simply say "Don't worry about it …you can't control it, and anyway it will all come out right in the end."

Now this is so stupid and so disingenuous, I refuse to dignify it with commentary. Except I must say it simply isn't so, and whoever believes it is living in a fool's delusion. Yes, dying is inevitable for everyone, but the Christian faith says what happens after death does not necessarily come out fine and may not be a good time for everyone. Death may indeed be simply death; the end. Or it may be the doorway to heaven. Or it may be the doorway to hell.

Christian theology agrees the world will come to an end because it is the inescapable result of the fact of Sin. As Paul put it, "the sting of Sin is death." But as we have seen, God has provided the antidote for sin, and thus for death. Those who are in Christ do not die. There is no despair for them because there is no death. To despair is to die. To be in Christ is to live. To despair, to deny hope, leads to hell. To live in faith is to be in heaven.

If we are honest, we cannot debate or even discuss the end of the world in an abstract way for what we are really talking about is the end to our personal life. And that is impossible to discuss in an uninvolved manner.

It may be uncomfortable and upsetting to talk about it, but beyond that we simply cannot actually conceive of our own end! Oh, intellectually we realize we are going to die ... but existentially we don't completely believe it! Our death is an incomprehensible concept for us because we are alive; and being alive we are not able to conceive of not being alive.

I was part of the study group at Billings Hospital in Chicago in the middle 1960's which led to Dr. Elizabeth Kubler Ross's landmark book, "On Death and Dying". Dr. Ross was on staff at the hospital. Most hospitals at that time offered little to nothing to patients who were dying. The thrust of medicine, after all, was to heal.

But Billings Hospital had an active program of clinical pastoral care in which I participated; and Dr. Ross allowed us to be involved in her case studies with terminal patients. We met in groups in which they discussed the approaching end of their life.

This led to her book in which she delineates her famous five stages of dealing with death "denial, feeling of isolation, anger, bargaining, depression, and finally acceptance."

What struck me, as I was there as an observer, was the inability for those in the process of dying to really understand that THEY were dying. It was more like they were discussing the death of a person called "Me," somewhat from a distance, more like someone watching the process, not participating in it.

Other than as an intellectual construct, "My" death is impossible to accept because it demands that I admit I am not in control of my life. To admit that life is a gift given to me, not something achieved by me is hard to do. So, many prefer the other choice; to see death as a foreign power coming to take life away from us. Here is where whether we are people of faith or not comes powerfully into play.

If we are people of faith, we will focus on the fact that life is a gift that was given to us. If we are not people of faith, we likely focus upon the fact that life is being taken from us. And in that we find the difference between worldly realism and the Christian faith.

The world will end: a bang, a whimper, whatever way it happens, it will come to an end and will all be over. The Christian faith insists, however, the end will be followed by a new creation. It will not be all over; it will just be a new beginning.

We do not know the mind of God as to the how this new creation will come about, but the why is very clear; from the beginning, God had both plan and purpose for creation. In the long history of Israel, the plan of God was kept alive in the promise of the Messiah who would come and in him the purpose God intended from the beginning would be fulfilled.

In Jesus God entered time and history to bring about that long intended purpose. God becoming human changed both time and history forever.

In Jesus, the chaos and probability which had determined life, and would have continued to do so, was replaced with love and grace. And the death of creation, in an uncertain but probable fiery end that would last forever, has been replaced with a new heaven and earth, and human annihilation replaced with resurrection to continued eternal life.

All of this was in God's mind from the beginning and all of it is made known to us only by revelation. But, darn, none of this is considered credible to a world that denies the validity of revelation!

This book however is about the Christian Faith, and in the Christian faith God's revelation is the foundation upon which everything is based, from the first statement in Genesis, "In the beginning God created..." to the last statement in the book of Revelation; "Behold I make all things new!"

For the Christian faith the end of the world, and death, which is the end of the world for the person dying, is an ending in order to bring forth a new beginning. Until the end arrives, we live in a tension between this world, in which the glory of God is veiled and the righteousness of God seems compromised, and the world to come, where the whole meaning of life and history will be revealed.

However, all of that is so huge it can only be symbolized. We can only try to describe the indescribable and realize that the result will be more the product of our own imagination than anything else. We can't know what we do not know. We cannot know what is yet to be. The Christian faith asserts that nonetheless we can know, utterly and certainly, that in the midst of all that is, and ever will be, we are each of us held tightly within the love of the almighty God of creation who bids us call him Father.

And we can know that all things are within God's power. And on that day to come, whenever, whatever, however, we shall be with God in a way that fulfills and completes the intention he has had, as Peter put it, " from before the foundation of the world." (1 Peter 1:20)

20

The Trinity

Now here we come to a really difficult concept!

Years ago I was teaching theology at a Rhode's Scholar event and tried to explain the Trinity. When I finished, having done my best, a lady came up to me and said, "All my life I have never understood the Trinity. I still don't." She is not alone.

Ideally the theology of the church is based upon God's revelation in the Old and New Testaments, and for the greater part that is true. But only "the greater part," not the whole of it, for too often when revelation does not adequately explain something, human arrogance will attempt to fill in the perceived gap. And that is what has produced many theological doctrines, which actually have little or no basis in the understanding of God in the Bible.

It was revelation that brought the first understanding of God to early Judaism. The conviction that there is only one God is set forth in the "Shema," "Hear O

Israel, the lord our God is one Lord." (Deut.6:4) Called monotheism, this is the very first revelation God gave regarding himself..."I am the Lord, there is none else, there is no God beside me." (Isaiah 45:5)

The second revelation of God regarding himself comes to us in Jesus. In the Christian faith "Christology" is the term for the effort to understand the essence of the person Jesus, his nature, human and divine, and his place in the plan and purpose of God.

For the writers of the New Testament there was no question Jesus was the Son of God. But the Gospels, and Paul, differ in the degree or manner in which this was so. It was not a doubting of the fact but an uncertainty of the "mix"...how much of Jesus was God, therefore divine, and how much was human?

And there was the equally important question: Was Jesus equal to the Father or was he subordinate? What was the relationship between the two? And how does the Holy Spirit enter in?

What was to become "The doctrine of the Trinity" was at first an unsettled uncertainty. However, a Trinitarian understanding did exist in the community as early as the year 110 when Ignatius of Antioch referred to God as being composed of the "Father, Christ Jesus and the Holy Spirit".

And another early church leader, Justin Martyr, not quite a generation later, ended one of his letters, "in the name of God, the Father and Lord of the universe, and of our Savior Jesus Christ, and of the Holy Spirit." So the concept of a trinity of persons in the Godhead was present very early in the church.

It was not a defined doctrine though, and so it continued to be debated in the Councils of Nicaea 325, Constantinople 381, and finally Chalcedon 451.

The Chalcedon council accepted the Nicene Creed with the clause. "I believe in the Holy Spirit, the Lord, the giver of life, who proceeds from the Father and the Son, who with the Father and the Son is worshipped and glorified." This settled it for the Western part of the church: the Roman Catholic Church, the Anglican and Protestant churches.

It was not settled in the churches in the Eastern part of the empire, however, who insisted that the Spirit proceeds from the Father through the Son. This difference was then, and remains now, a major divergence between Eastern and Western Christianity.

That may sound like splitting hairs, as we say, and in some respect it is. But to be honest, the whole doctrine of the Trinity is somewhat problematic, and perhaps both views are right. Then again, maybe neither is right. In the end perhaps we ought to say the doctrine of the Trinity is not a fully completed doctrine but remains an incomplete way to understand the reality that is God.

Now that may very well be astutely true, but it would be a hard statement to sell when we consider the fact that as historians Will and Ariel Durant relate in their book, "The Age of Faith," in the early centuries of the church more Christians killed each other in disputes over the Trinity than were martyred by Rome.

That fact should result in remorse and humility and the realization that all theological understanding is at best imperfect and only, in Paul's words, "a reflection in a poor mirror" of what is really true about God.

My opinion is that the doctrine of the Trinity is a confusion that is both exciting in its demands, unrequited in its fulfillment, and in the end a mystery beyond our comprehension. So why do we believe it, or try to believe it? Why is it such an issue in the church?

The continued use of the symbol of the Trinity in the church is because as believers we have come to know God's presence among us in three somewhat distinct ways; God our Creator, Jesus our Redeemer, and the Holy Spirit our Guide and Comforter.

These are real experiences in our lives and were as well in the life of the early church. Ultimately they led to the concept of God as a Trinity, three persons in one being. Existentially, far more than an abstract doctrine, the Trinity is a personal reality that wraps itself around us every minute of life.

We will look at that personal perspective in the next chapter "the Apostles Creed."

21

The Apostles Creed

The Apostles Creed is a statement of the Christian faith. It is what we believe. It is how we see things, how we understand life and the world. It is a way of saying we do not, cannot, look at the world as do those who do not believe. From the perspective of a Christian the eyes of an unbeliever are myopic. They are cataract-covered eyes or blind eyes. At any rate eyes that simply do not see clearly.

Unbelievers only think they see things as they really are; in truth they miss the deeper reality. Christians see with the eyes of faith, a gift given to us. And it is by faith and only by faith, that we can say the articles of the Creed.

The First Article

"I believe in God, the father almighty, creator of heaven and earth…."

The intention of the creed is to make it clear it is not merely by chance that we exist. Not only the universe, but each one of us is a deliberate creation by God because he loves us and wants us to live in relationship with him.

To say "Creator of heaven and earth" not only means God did create in the past but more importantly continues to do it now as new galaxies, possibly new universes, come into existence every day. And of the greatest importance, God is also the creator of every new child that is born.

To call this creator "Father" is to say I believe the love of God….creating, loving, fatherly, motherly love …has come to me and is caring and active in my life right now. That is what we are saying when we say I believe in God the father almighty.

This means that God who is creator, who is the Father, is also the Lord of life and death. God owns life and death. He controls it. God who can speak the word of life can also, even in the midst of the mighty achievements and proud accomplishment of human life, speak the sentence of death and none can ignore it. "You fool," says the parable, "tonight your life will be required of you, and whose will be all these accomplishments?" (Luke 12: 20)

God can not only speak the word that gives life, or the word that brings death, but into the midst of the meaninglessness and doom that hangs over human life, God can speak the creative word that says, "Live again, be born once more." None other can say that; none other has control over that, only the one who is the Almighty Creator.

The point of this first article is to make it clear we live unconditionally in the hands of God, who has us completely in his power. God is the creator; we are the created. But the unexpected joy in this article is that the creator is not an abstract entity but God is Father to his creation. That is what it means to say "I believe in God the father almighty, creator of heaven and earth."

Second Article

…"and in Jesus Christ, His only Son Our Lord…"

Jesus is the presence of God among us. Jesus is God's son, and always behind Jesus, within Jesus, empowering him, upholding him, is God the Father.

The Creed then states that Jesus "was conceived by the Holy Spirit, born of the Virgin Mary…" If we get caught in the particulars of this statement we risk losing the intent and meaning of it; that Jesus, being conceived by the Spirit, is true God, and being born of Mary, is also true man.

That is an incredible assertion, and before it we ask the same question Mary did, "How can this be?" Well, the angel answered her, and answers us: "The Holy Spirit will come upon you, and the power of the Most High will cover you. For this reason the baby will be holy and will be called the Son of God."
(Luke 1:35)

The Creed makes the very probable assumption Mary was a virgin when Jesus was conceived. Not concerned about the process of that conception, the intent of the creed is to say Jesus did not owe his existence to only human factors. Neither Mary nor Joseph, no human being, decided Jesus should be born is the point. God alone wanted him, determined him, and gave him existence.

Whatever means God used to do that, whether Joseph was the biological father or not, Jesus is a direct, intentional, creative act of God. He is God come among us, and the inconceivable truth in this birth is that through Mary, in Jesus, God literally becomes one of us.

The creed continues, "....suffered under Pontius Pilate was crucified, died and was buried."

In Jesus God took on the powers of evil, death and destruction, using no weapons but truth and love. And he lost. He was defeated. This is seriously important...Jesus, who was born as we are born, flesh as we are flesh, contended against evil with all his power...and lost.

Being one of us, he lost, as we also lose. He lost and he suffered the consequences. Rome crucified him. The cross of Jesus is the climax of the constant battle which has reigned from the beginning of history between good and evil, right and wrong. Jesus suffered as mankind has always suffered at the hands of the powers of the world. The whole epic battle of good vs. evil is concentrated in that one phrase "...suffered under Pontius Pilate, was crucified, died and was buried."

This is the truth that makes us fall to our knees in amazement and awe. The love of God was so deep, so complete, so resolute that God sends his son who consciously and deliberately walks into the darkness of death.

And Jesus dies in utter loneliness. Jesus' death was the actual end of his life. There was no soul or spirit that remained. He died. And he was buried. It was over. He was dead. And he descended to hell, or in the ecumenical version, "he descended to the dead."

Jesus was truly human, one of us. And taking our sin upon himself, like us he too was doomed to death, extinction. There is no life after death; dead is dead. There is nothing in us or within us that lives on after death. When we die we are dead.

So also like us, Jesus died and he was buried. And Jesus descended to the place of the dead. Jesus died and he ceased to exist. Let that roll around in your head! That's what it means that Jesus was truly human.

Then the creed continues; "On the third day he rose from the dead." God who is the Lord of life, who creates life, gives life, gave life again to Jesus. And he joins his father in heaven.

The Third Article

"I believe in the Holy Spirit; the holy Christian Church, the communion of saints; the forgiveness of sins; the resurrection of the body; and the life everlasting." The third article makes it clear that all that has been said up to this point is not abstract theological theory but a personal fact for each of us.

So when we say we believe in the Holy Spirit, it is to say we believe all the statements which follow: the Church, which is the communion of saints in which we live, the forgiveness of sins which is what makes us a saint, and the resurrection of the body and life everlasting, which is ours because we live in Jesus and receive it from God as Jesus did.

The Creed in Summary

The Spirit comes to us from God and takes residence within us. The Spirit comes to us through the Word and the Sacraments and brings us into the community of the church where, together with others, we become the communion of saints, a member of the fellowship which extends around the world, and down through the centuries.

Science is now telling us that the past is part of the present; it is not gone and forgotten but is influencing and active in our lives...not simply in a DNA and genetic sense, but in a very real spiritual sense, as the psychiatrist Karl Jung tried so hard to show us.

We are part of the spiritual heritage of the church. We could say I believe because my mother believed.... grandfather ...someone I never knew 500 years ago believed. In other words, I believe because the communion of saints has preserved the faith and the gospel and passed it on to me.

Actually the Apostles Creed is less a statement of faith than it is a living proclamation of the Gospel which is behind it, within it and all around it. The good news is that God loves, forgives, and accepts us in Jesus Christ.

The Nicene Creed and Athanasian Creeds

These two creedal statements are later documents in the church dealing with theological issues that arose in debate between the Western and Eastern Church. We no longer think in the philosophical categories of that time, and the two creeds have become largely ignored.

Very briefly, the Nicene Creed provides a fuller description of God's creation "…all that is, seen and unseen." And of Jesus…"true God… begotten, not made, and of one being with the father," who through the agency of the Holy Spirit became incarnate from the Virgin Mary. There is no descent into hell! The statement, "I believe in the Holy Spirit" is also expanded.

The Athanasian Creed takes its name from Athanasius, the great theologian of the Fourth Century, but the creed itself dates from the Sixth Century, deriving from the conflicts between the Eastern and Western churches.

The statements of this Creed go way beyond the other two to make it clear God's Son and the Holy Spirit are of one being with the Father; and that Jesus Christ is true God and a true human being in one person.

The importance of these two creeds is beyond the purpose of this book and would require one in itself, but they, together with the Apostles Creed, are the foundation symbols of the Christian Faith!

22

The Lord's Prayer

Does prayer work? And, of even more importance to each of us, will MY prayer work?

The heart of our problem is the doubts and questions prayer brings into our mind. To question the value of prayer and whether it really makes a difference is reasonable, and we can't escape it. However, we must remember God raised Jesus from death which shows us who is really in charge of this world!

Knowing the risen Lord is our advocate and confidant, we can have a heart-to-heart conversation with our heavenly Father about how things are going in our life.

Heart-to-heart because God does not stand on formalities but prefers we take our shoes off and get comfortable. Prayer is not imposing on him. We are family. So forget formality and pray "Dad...Mom." Prayer is that personal. To pray is to enter a world in which the embrace of God is so real and true it is felt deeply in our soul. We are never as close to God as we are in prayer.

Don't get caught in that seductive doubt that if we haven't prayed for some time God will hold it against us. We are quite inventive and can come up with lots of reasons why we are not worthy and therefore God might not listen. But that is nonsense. We are God's beloved children; we can trust in that and just pray.

Let prayer be what it is: a very personal conversation between each of us and God. Prayer is what happens when we stop talking about God and talk to God. When we are sincerely in prayer we put ourselves into God's hands and we feel the grip of God holding us. It's powerful stuff and it does work miracles and change things.

Because God is our father/our mother, we are therefore in a family relationship; and our prayers will be answered in a result that is good and right for us. However, while God hears and listens to our prayers, we do not always see our needs clearly enough to know what is best and right for us to ask, even as we fervently pray for what we desire.

So our Father's answer is not always what we want, but rather what we should want, what we need, what

is the best and right thing for us. The Spirit helps us to bend our prayers and turn our will to God's will.
Does prayer work when we pray for people we don't even know as in prayer chains or public prayers on civic occasions? This is a difficult question to answer, but the answer is: yes....no....sometimes....maybe.

In a carefully crafted empirical study, patients with very similar conditions were divided into two groups. One group was prayed for by prayer chains and the other group was not. There was no difference in the result of those who were prayed for and those who were not. I am not sure what this study really shows.

For the secular world it shows prayer is merely mumbling because there is no God out there who cares. The cynical certainty is that since there are millions of planets in our universe and perhaps thousands of universes, how can one person matter? That is reasonable, and it is an inescapable point of view if we are not living in relationship with God. It is only when we know there is someone who hears and cares that we can pray.

Jesus prayed unceasingly. And watching him at prayer every day his disciples asked him one day, "Lord teach us how to pray." He gave them what we call "The Lord's Prayer." He gave the prayer to his disciples; and truly, only the Christian community is able to address God as:

Our Father…

Father is not a gender description of God. It is a familial one. Jesus includes his followers in the family of God, giving them permission to approach God in the same way he does.

Think about it. You and I…we dare to be that familiar with God. But only in Jesus! In Jesus we are family; and because we are in God's family we can begin our prayer, should begin our prayer, "Dad, Mom…"

…who art in heaven…

We acknowledge that God, although as close to us as a father, is still the Lord of the Universe. He is, as Isaiah said, "high and lifted up." God is not a kindly soft touch daddy or mommy. God reigns over all that is, he created it, maintains it, and has the power over everything as he rules from his throne in heaven. Therefore immediately we must say:

…hallowed be your name.
To use God's name is an awesome thing and even

though, in Jesus, we come before one who loves us, with whom we can thus be very familial, we dare not forget we come before the Holy Ruler of the Universe! God is the one who is all things, has all power, one whom it is our duty to...honor and serve, obey and regard with reverence. To hallow God's name is to make it holy, and so our prayer quickly acknowledges that God is holy.

The Greek form of the word "hallowed" is active mode which means we don't just say "hallowed be." We are to bring it about by what we do in the world to make it holy and to show to the world that God IS holy.

We are family, we regard each other in love, and we are to be protective of the family name. We are not, says the commandment, to take the name of the Lord in vain but keep it holy. God's name is hallowed in God's kingdom where it is praised and said with joy and gratitude. But we are to also keep it holy in the world where it is not typically so regarded. In the world God's Kingdom is not a full reality, so we pray:

Thy Kingdom come ...

In Jesus' resurrection the kingdom of God has come among us and we who are in Christ are living in the

Kingdom now. Therefore, in this petition we do not so much pray for the kingdom of God to come in the world ...but rather we are asking, in the sense that Luther understood this petition, that it come to me and to all people, who hunger and thirst for what the kingdom of this world cannot provide.

The things of God are not fully provided in this world because we are all caught in bondage to our own will. We put ourselves and our desires above those of God. So we must pray ...

Thy will be done ... on earth

"I have come," said Jesus, "to do the will of my father who sent me." Jesus was here to do God's will. In the garden of Gethsemane he prayed, "Not my will but thine be done." We pray the same words in the Lord's Prayer.

Jesus was not fatalistically submitting to the events about to take place. He was not praying for deliverance, even more he was not praying for calm and peace in the midst of things he could not understand. He was praying for the will of God to be done because he knew, with a sure and certain knowledge that beat in his heart and filled every nerve in his body, that God's will is good and right. And therefore he prays that it be done....on earth!

Jesus was clear that suffering, death, and terror are NOT God's will. God does not will them. They are not part of a great plan God has in mind. To the world this may seem a possibility; that God is, at worst, a sadistic monster who wills death and destruction, or, at best, a weakling with no power to change anything. Simply looking at life as one who is caught in it, this seems a reasonable point of view.

Not however to one who lives in a relationship of trust with God. When the love and grace of God has enwrapped our lives, we can see the terrors and fears of life from a totally different perspective. Living in Christ Jesus we know God's will is always to do the best for us. It's completely a matter of trust. Trust in our relationship with God. But we are not to simply bask in that certainty…

….as it is in Heaven …

Only after we pray, "they will be done ...on earth," can we add, "as it is in heaven." In God's eternal kingdom his will is done, completely and unequivocally done. But on earth it is not, it is opposed at every turn. So we pray that God's will be done on earth as well as in heaven.

By us!

That ultimately is really the point. As we have seen in earlier chapters, the earth and human history is the scene of the struggle between God, the world, and the flesh. Two powers waging war...light and darkness, good and evil, God and Satan. This is a real situation.

And into this situation comes the Lord's Prayer telling us we are not to simply capitulate. We are not to passively go along, say it's more than I can handle...no, we are to pray that God's will be done on earth, by us.

We pray that God give us the strength, give us the spirit, to do what we can, whenever and however we can, to bring about God's kingdom on earth. As the old popular song put it, "Little things mean a lot." We make a difference when we make a difference.

The Lord's Prayer reminds us that the horror of this world is due to the powers of Evil, not to God. We cannot find God's will everywhere in the world; what

The Lord's Prayer reminds us that the horror of this world is due to the powers of Evil, not to God. We cannot find God's will everywhere in the world; what we find are examples of incredible goodness and incredible evil. A battle is waging between the two.
And we are not to sit by the side of the road and do nothing. We are not to passively accept what comes. Jesus never said to a sick man, "Accept your sickness ... be happy in your blindness, and praise God for your health." He never said, "Love your troubles for they are God's will "...no, he reached out and cured, he showed that God is opposed to sickness, to evil, to sin.

In Jesus we see the heart of God; we see the will of God. Only in Jesus do we, can we, know that, yes, all things do work for good ... and I must work for it as well.

Give us this day our daily bread…

"Daily" is what you might call a "best guess." The original Greek word in both gospels is "epiousios," which is used nowhere else in the Greek world. Very unusual, Jesus coined the word. What Jesus meant by it, or what Matthew or Luke meant by it, is a guess.

Scholars guess "daily" because bread in the average household was consumed daily; it did not keep and had to be made each day. The supposed meaning is that God give us sustenance for today that we may not be in want and may have the strength to do his will and advance his kingdom.

Forgive us our sins as we forgive...

Wouldn't you know, one little word in Jesus' prayer has caused endless controversy in the church? Jesus said forgive us "as" we forgive others. We have generally misunderstood this to mean we are forgiven "as," or in the same way, or to the same degree, that we forgive others. But that IS a misunderstanding. The intention of this petition is to tell us that we must ask forgiveness for ourselves "so that" we can forgive others as we have been forgiven.

Forgiveness comes first to us and in gratitude we are enabled to forgive others. Jesus is very clear in many places that forgiveness can only come to those who will also forgive.

And Jesus also made it clear that to forgive means to forgive as God forgives us and let go of all things committed against us. To forgive is to truly let it go as if it never happened. It doesn't work to say, "I can forgive but I can't forget." No, to forgive means to forget, to put it behind us, forget it entirely, be at peace with that decision, and move on. Only then, only when that has been done, can we ourselves be forgiven.

This is pretty deep but it is a needful thing to understand. We can only be forgiven if we forgive. Not because God will forgive only if we forgive, but because only a forgiving spirit can accept forgiveness. You have to know what it is to accept it!

…and lead us not into temptation…

The word Jesus uses for temptation is a very ambiguous word; the closest true meaning seems to be "trial." Do not bring us to the time of trial in the sense of a time of suffering, grief, pain, loss, persecution. Like Jesus in the garden, we pray, "Father, keep this from us." We do not want pain or suffering; we do not want to lose our loved ones...we do not want these things to happen. And yet we must trust that God who loves us will bring good and blessing out of all evil and pain that befalls us. This is a mighty big test of our faith, but we need to believe that, because only when we believe that can we say...

…but deliver us from evil…

As Peter put it, Satan is "prowling around like a roaring lion seeking whom to devour." In a world that does not do God's will, in a world where God's will is thwarted and laughed at every day…constantly and everywhere…in a world that is caught in the grasp of evil, we pray to be delivered from it.

It is not only God's will that is at work on earth. There is another will, an opposing power. There is one actively striving against the will of God. In the First Century this evil force was personalized as Satan, never meant to be literally understood, but rather a symbol or a metaphor for evil. Just as Santa Claus is a symbol or metaphor for Christmas joy and love, so Satan was the metaphor for evil. And because, as we all know well, evil is personal and not an abstract concept, Satan was presented as a real being.

Now that is a profound and real truth. But we have lost that understanding; and there are many today who argue that not only is there no Satan, there is no evil power at all. They argue there is no evil, only evil deeds. Well, the Christian faith disavows that. The Lord's Prayer denies that and recognizes the reality of evil and asks God to keep it from us.

For thine is the kingdom, the power and the glory forever. …..

In Jesus we see the heart of God; we see the will of God, and we know that, yes, all things do work to the end they should. To God belongs the kingdom.

(This "doxology" is omitted in three of the most important ancient manuscripts in existence and appears to have been unknown in much of the early community. In the Roman Catholic version it is not included. For Protestants it is in the prayer because Martin Luther added it in the 15th century. It most likely was not in Jesus' original version.)

23

Other Religions

While our concern in this book is the Christian Faith, we must consider at least briefly the essential and overarching similarities and disagreements between Christianity and other religious faiths.

And what about those three always-with-us questions:

1. Are Christians right and all others wrong?

2. Does it matter what you believe, as long as you believe?

3. Are all religions equal?

The short answer is no, yes, and no. And yet it is amazing to me that Jesus is not an unknown person in any religion, all of which have some place for him in their faith. This is an indirect way of dealing with the question of whether what God has done in Jesus is the only door to salvation, or whether God is working equally among all the other religions of the world to achieve the same purpose.

In other words, are those who come to Jesus...more accurately, are brought to Jesus by the Holy Spirit... the only ones saved? Or will God somehow save people who do not know Jesus, and who are not part of the Christian community of faith? St. Paul said a wife's faith can save her husband who does not believe, so why not simply extend that inclusion?
(1 Corinthians 7:14)

We who have been brought to faith by God's love and grace know that it is not on the basis of goodness, strong faith, or anything else that we have been chosen. It is not our deserving but purely a matter of God's grace. So personal experience has taught us it is best to just leave the question of who will be saved in God's hands.

Our journey to the kingdom, our life experience in this world, has surely shown us we cannot say that Christians alone are right, or that others are wrong. And even more than personal experience, we must hesitate in judgement because the future of the world is incomplete and unknown.

The day of the Lord has not yet come and only on

that day will we see who has been called, who has been saved. And we will be surprised, says the book of Revelations, that on that day those who are before God's throne come from all nations and races and tongues.

Having said that, it must also be said the Christian faith maintains the future of humanity has already arrived among us in Jesus of Nazareth. And that whoever is to be saved will, by the grace and mercy of God, in some way come to the kingdom through Christ. This is a viewpoint unique to Christianity.

With that in mind, we will briefly contrast the Christian faith with the Jewish, Muslim, Buddhist, Hindu and Mormon faiths. Also, we will consider Secularism and Atheism. As we proceed, please realize that there are nuances to every faith which would likely at least to some degree modify the main tenets presented here.

Still, all religions have in common the use of rituals and doctrines and theology to explain the faith, and relate the things of God to the everyday life of their followers. And all religions gather the faithful into groups or units in which they are taught and in which they offer praise and worship to God.

Most religions also have a Holy Book which is the authority for the faith. Christians have the Hebrew Bible and the New Testament, in which we believe the essentials of the faith have been written down for our guidance. Jews have the Hebrew Bible, formerly called the Old Testament.

The Holy Books of each religion raise very important qualifications and concerns for any effort of one religion to understand another. In a sense all religions are speaking about the same subject: God, the Holy, Buddha, Allah; but are doing so from different perspectives. Unfortunately this almost insures there will be disagreement and arguments about not only God but everything the religion teaches.

There are three large problems that face any discussion:

The first problem in discussing religion is that each religion differs about what is important and what is necessary for faith or salvation and do not always mean the same things by the words used.

The second problem is that each religion believes passionately that it is the true faith. It may not consider other faiths to be wrong, but certainly does regard them as being lesser to their own.

The third problem is that not every adherent of the religion…be it Christian, Buddhist, Muslim, Hindu or Mormon…believes everything their religion espouses or believes in the same way. Among different believers in each religion there will be differing views of what is true and not true, what is of ultimate importance, little importance, or no real importance at all.

As we have seen in the radical jihadists, the more passionate a believer is about his or her faith, the stronger is the likelihood they will feel the necessity to preach the true word and convert others to the true faith. And the more passionately one believes in his or her faith, the more profoundly the differences with other faiths matter to that person and can lead into a consuming antagonism and even hatred of other religious views.

Nonetheless, keep in mind that the whole human family is united in the incredible and wonderful fact that we are all children of God; and that even though our faith differs in how we realize that, we are all held within the love and grace of God the Father. Thus we have more in common than not!

In the next chapters we look at the extended family of God: Judaism, Islam, Buddhist, Hindu and Mormon.

And those outside the family of faith but still loved by God: Atheists, Agnostics and Secularists.

24

Judaism

Judaism is the oldest of the three faiths which spring from the Patriarch Abraham: Judaism, Christianity and Islam. Its most basic and fundamental beliefs arise from the Hebrew Bible, and in particular, from the first five books: Genesis, Exodus, Leviticus, Numbers and Deuteronomy.

Those five books, known as the "Torah" are the most significant and authoritative religious texts in Judaism. They contain 613 commandments which, in great detail, instruct Jews how to live a God pleasing life. They give God's sacred revelations and confirm God's commitment to Jews as the chosen people.

The years following the destruction of the Second Temple in 70 C.E. ended the previous divisions of religious leadership, which had been present during the time of Jesus: the Pharisees, Sadducees, and Scribes that we are so familiar with in the New Testament. Those divisions fell away and what is today called Rabbinic Judaism emerged.

That was a huge change, but what proved to be even more important, with the change came
the radical decision that the Torah cannot be properly understood without referring to the Oral Law (the Mishnah), which can only be properly interpreted by the Rabbis. This often led to acrimony, for not everyone agreed with the interpretations brought forth by this Rabbi or that Rabbi.

The result was the formation of three branches: Orthodox, Conservative, and Reform, further subdivided by varieties of interpretation of the Torah.

Orthodox Judaism

The smallest of the three, about 10 per cent of all Jews, it is also the most traditional of the three. Orthodoxy believes that God literally gave the Torah to Moses, and therefore its rules are divine and must be obeyed. So without question all 613 commandments in the Torah are binding on all Jews.

In Orthodox worship there often is a barrier between men and women at services called a mechitza. There can be no Orthodox women rabbis. Orthodox Jews must observe the Sabbath and keep kosher laws. Orthodoxy is the only recognized Judaism in Israel.

Conservative Judaism

Conservative Judaism, comprising about 40% of Jews, agrees with the Orthodox that all 613 commandments of the law are binding, including keeping the Sabbath, keeping kosher, and utilizing a considerable amount of Hebrew in the synagogue services.

Then, in departure from the Orthodox Jews who maintain the Law, once given, is for all time, Conservative Jews believe it is evolving as humans learn more about how to interpret the Torah. On this basis conservative Jews have changed some of the Orthodox interpretations. For example, men and women can worship together, people may ride in a car on the Sabbath to attend services, and women may be ordained as rabbis. While in theory all the religious laws are required, in practice many Conservative Jews are lax about observing them or obey them only in part.

Reform Judaism

Reform Jews compose the largest group of American Jews, about 50%. Reform Jews do not accept the binding nature of Jewish law, focusing instead on the moral autonomy of individuals to decide how the law is to be observed. In general, Reform Judaism is liberal. Keeping kosher is not required, and there is less Hebrew in worship services than in the Orthodox or Conservative services. However, there is some movement within contemporary Reform Judaism toward embracing some of the more traditional practices of the faith.

Intermarriage and conversion lift up the one place where differences in the 3 branches really become important. Especially for American Jews, intermarriage and conversion are burning issues.

Orthodox rabbis refuse to perform intermarriages without an Orthodox conversion first and do not recognize conversions performed by non-Orthodox rabbis.

Conservative rabbis will neither perform nor attend a marriage between someone born Jewish and an unconverted Gentile. They do generally recognize the conversions and marriages performed by other rabbis as long as the proper ritualistic requirements have been met.

Reform Judaism usually has no requirements for inter-faith marriage, and rabbis officiate without them. Not surprising, Reform Judaism has both the largest number of converts and intermarried families of all three divisions.

Conservative and Orthodox branches follow the matrilineal principle that a person is Jewish only if that person's mother is Jewish or if that person converts to Judaism.

Reform Judaism believes that children of a Jewish father and Gentile mother are Jewish if the child is brought up as Jewish and publicly identifies as a Jew. He or she does not need to convert in order to be Jewish.

****

Technically there is a fourth branch of Judaism, known as Reconstructionist. This exists only in the United States where it was started in the last century by Mordecai Kaplan. Very liberal, rejecting the concept of Jews as a chosen people, it makes up barely 3% of American Jews. So, in a very general sense, we have very conservative Jews in Israel, very liberal, in the United States.

Differences and similarities with the Christian Faith

Both Judaism and Christianity regard the Hebrew Bible -- the Old Testament -- as the document which bears witness to the beginning of God's saving work in history. We worship the same God and hold many ethical concerns in common, and in an essential sense, disagree in faith only on Jesus of Nazareth as the Messiah.

This is a disagreement important enough to raise the question whether Jews are saved through their covenant relationship with God or whether they must accept Jesus. A 50-50 split among theologians of mainline Christian denominations leaves room for lots of conversation!

One side of this conversation is called "The Two Covenant Theory of Salvation." Basically, it says God has established two different, but equally valid, covenants; the old one with Israel and the new covenant, as Jesus called it, with Christians. The Covenant in Moses and the Covenant in Jesus are both regarded as being valid. So in this view Jews are saved in and by their Jewish faith.

The other side holds that the same requirement applies for Jews as for all of us; salvation comes through Jesus Christ. Then, considering that the Jews are and have always been the "chosen people," it is in God's hands how or in what way that requirement will be applied.

So, while ultimately up to God, during the "between times" in which we are living, Christians continue to have a special relationship with Jews. They are part of the same household of faith and are literally all brothers and sisters in Jesus, Abraham and Sarah. The bridge or bond we share with Jews when we confess our faith is that we both pray to Yahweh whom Jesus called Abba.

And yet there is a difference between Christians and Jews. For Christians, Jesus is the Messiah promised of Old in the Hebrew Scriptures and history of the Jewish people. For Jews, Jesus was another prophet and they still wait for the Messiah, God's entrance into human events, and the bringing of a new heaven and a new earth.

So, as we pray in thanksgiving that the Messiah has come in Jesus, they continue to pray that the Messiah will come. The concern for the Messiah unites us like family members, but as is often true in families, it is also the dividing difference between us.

Happily, St. Paul says this division is only temporary and he makes it clear in Romans that in the end all Jews will come to understand and acknowledge

Jesus as the Messiah, something which he says is in God's plan, though not apparent to us. (Romans 11:25-26)

For roughly 50% of Christian theologians, there is no reason for a practicing Jew to convert to Christianity, since God's original covenant with Jews remains intact. And there is no reason for us to try to convert them since we are both in the same family and one day will be reunited.

25

Islam

For many non-Muslims, the term Allah, the Arabic name of God, refers to some distant and strange deity worshiped only by Arabs. However, in Arabic, the word Allah means the One True God. Therefore, in Islamic understanding even Jews and Christians can refer to the Supreme Being as Allah.

In Islam, a human being is not a sinful creature in need of redemption but a being that still carries an imprint of God on his/her soul which lies deeply buried under layers of negligence. Humans are not born sinful, but forgetful. There is no need for redemption, only illumination to bring to mind what they innately know but do not remember. (In the early Christian community this view was a sub-category within a heresy known as Gnosticism)

Islamic doctrine holds that men and women still carry deep down within their souls the knowledge that this universe has a Creator. This is instinctive and therefore requires no proof. You know it when you see it. However, some do not see it, especially in the

West where debasing culture reduces and eliminates this innate belief and confuses the person.

The God of Islam, Allah, Is the Supreme Lord of heaven and earth. He is the Lord of every man, woman, and child, which means they belong exclusively to Him. He alone brought existence out of non-existence, and all existence depends on him for its conservation and continuance.

Islam agrees with Christianity that Allah did not create the universe and then leave it to pursue its own course according to fixed laws, thereafter ceasing to take any further interest in it. No, in Islam the power of the Living God is required at every moment to sustain all creatures. Creation has no Lord besides Him. Allah is also the only Ruler of the affairs of men.

Allah is also the Absolute Judge, the Legislator, and he alone distinguishes right from wrong. What is required of believers is that they surrender to God's will and worship him. (Not much difference here from Christianity.)

Allah's right to be worshiped cannot be over-emphasized; it is the essential meaning of Islam's testimony of faith. Islam insists that every act, belief, statement, or sentiment--everything that brings a person closer to the Creator--is true worship of God. This includes "external" worship like the daily ritual prayers, fasting, charity, and pilgrimage and the "internal" worship of faith, reverence, adoration, love, gratitude, and reliance.

Allah is to be worshiped with all the body, soul, and heart. However, worship is incomplete unless it is done out of four essential elements: reverential fear of God, divine love and adoration, hope in divine reward, and extreme humility.

Islam firmly believes that Allah divinely revealed books to his prophets to guide mankind. The Quran is not the only spoken Word of God, for Allah also spoke to prophets before Prophet Muhammad; "...and to Moses God spoke directly." (Quran 4:164) Islam maintains that prophets were sent by God throughout the ages to lead human beings to Him. They accept Abraham as one of those prophets, and Jesus as well. But above this, in a special way, the Quran is God's MOST divine revelation, the definitive holy word of God.

If a person believes in Allah and follows His commandments, salvation and eternal happiness can be achieved by sincere worship. If one falls into sin, which is defined as pushing yourself away from the mercy of God, all that is required is sincere repentance which brings a person back to God.

The Quran is Allah's final revelation; it is sacred above sacred, as if it were Allah himself, and it applies for all of humankind-- all people, all times and places.

Islam rejects the basic principles of Christianity and states clearly that salvation is attained only through submission to the most merciful Allah. No Jesus accepted.

The Authorized Version of the Quran is composed of 114 chapters or suras, and each chapter has various numbers of verses or ayahs. There are 6,616 verses and 77,934 words. Strict Islam believers maintain every word was dictated to Mohammed by Gabriel, and thus is inspired in every word, every comma, and is in its entirety both infallible and without error.

Therefore, since the Quran is a holy book in that special sense, it cannot be touched by defiled hands which must be first be washed. It dare not be dropped, allowed to become dirty, or in any way disrespected. It is a holy book in the holiest sense for it is in no way the word of man but directly and completely the word of God.

The Quran for Islam holds the place of Christ for Christians, which is why they get so upset, even violent, when the Quran is mistreated. The Quran, the book itself, is the very presence of Allah for Islam.

However, there is a difficulty on the horizon. The Quran as we know it today is in reality two quite different books. The older Quran, the first eighty-six chapters were written in Mecca; the later one, 28 chapters, in Medina.

There is huge difference between the two. The Mecca Quran was all about tolerance, tranquility, spirituality, acceptance, and inner cleansing through submission to the word of Allah. In Medina, Mohammad's revelations became more and more assertive and violent as did his actions. There are really two Qurans...one peaceful and one not.

Now the importance of this is that Mohammed ruled that if a later saying contradicted a previous one, then the most recent was the true word of Allah. So the chronological order of the Quran is essential. But that is a problem, because the sayings are not in chronological order!

The more inclusive and open Muslim faith comes from the earlier Quran. The exclusionary and violence-condoning sayings come from the later Medina Quran; and being later, they supersede the peaceful intention of the earlier Mecca writings.

So, while Islam is a religion of peace, it is not a religion of peace. And one must be careful when accepting any quoting of the Quran. The relevance depends totally upon which part of the Quran it comes from.

How do Muslims decide whether to follow the peaceful or the jihadist verses? Well, in addition to the Quran, Islam has the hadith, Arabic for "tradition." It is a collection of teachings, deeds, and sayings of Muhammad as reported by his companions.

Essentially, these are sayings or opinions attributed to Muhammad, but not found in the Quran. The hadith (ha-deeth) is considered to be an essential clarification of the Quran and is considered to be just as holy.

The hadith collection is also called the Sunnah, or tradition, from which comes the term Sunni Muslims, or "traditional" Muslims Opposed to them are the Shi'ites, who broke away because they regarded Ali, the son-in-law of Muhammad, as the legitimate successor of Muhammad, and not the three caliphs who did succeed him.

Islam today is about 85% Sunni, 15% Shi'ite. The Sunni Muslims use the hadith, the musings of Muhammad, along with the Quran to interpret sharia, the moral and religious law of Islam. And it is from the hadith more than the Quran that the extremist views originate.

The hadith states that rewards of fighting in jihad are tremendous: "Allah guarantees him who strives in Jihad in the name of Allah that He will admit him into Paradise if martyred or if not, will bring him back to his dwelling place, with reward and booty." And those who are martyred, hadith says, will live in beautiful Gardens, and Allah shall say to them "O you who believe! Eat and drink because of your good deeds." (At-tur, Chapter #52, Verse #19)

"They will recline on carpets, whose inner linings will be of rich brocade: and they will have maidens, chaste and beautiful, whom no man before them has touched." (55:54-59) The number of virgins available comes from another of Muhammad's sayings. "The smallest reward in Paradise will be a palace over which will be a dome decorated with pearls, rubies and aquamarine, with 80,000 servants and 72 wives." (55: verse 72)

Pretty hard for the non-extremist or non-jihadists to argue against that! And then add that any kind of criticism of the Quran is forbidden because to question or defame the Quran is to do the same to God.

The Medina Muslims insist the Quran is infallible and inerrant in every way and that jihad is the responsibility of a true believer because infidels are to be obliterated. These Muslims, fundamentalists to the core, envision a regime based upon Sharia law and want to return the religion to exactly what it was in Medina in the 7th century. They prescribe death for apostasy, hanging for homosexuality, death by stoning for adultery.

It is Medina Muslim women who wear the burka and must live by a strict code of behavior. If they violate it, the husband's duty is to beat them for the infraction.

To a large degree American Muslims tend to think for themselves and generally lean toward the milder Mecca verses, while Arabs in the Middle East tend to follow what their tribe decides. If that is jihadist, they will probably follow along and become jihadist.

It's tough stuff Christians must face in dealing with Islam. But Islam is facing some tough stuff itself. The internet is opening up the religion of Islam to other views and opinions. For example, Western scholars point out that the Quran shows many additions and views from centuries later than the 7th, and therefore the Quran could not have been dictated to Mohammed in the way claimed, creating a real dilemma. No way to know what will come of it.

Comparison of Islam with Christianity

The Christian belief, that Jesus is the Son of God and is God, is rejected in Islam. Exalted Allah is above having a son, because to him belong all that is in the heavens and all that is in the earth.
(Quran 4:171)

The basis of the Christian Faith, that Jesus died on the cross for the sins of humankind and that salvation is received through belief in Jesus, is absolutely rejected in Islam. Jesus had one purpose, to reaffirm the message of the Prophets before him. The Quran says: "The Messiah Jesus, son of Mary, was a Messenger of God and His Word, which He bestowed on Mary and a spirit created by Him; so believe in God and His Messengers." (Quran 4:171) Islam acknowledges there was a plot to crucify Jesus but it did not succeed; he did not die but rather ascended into heaven. In the last days leading up to the Day of Judgement, Jesus will return to this world and spread the belief in the Oneness of God. At that time, he will also deny ever asking the people to worship him. And yet, at the same time, the Quran declares that Jesus is the Word and Truth of God, in the same way as Moses and David and the prophet Mohammad himself. (Quran 4:156-158)

The difference that matters is that salvation through Jesus is not required: every human being can attain salvation by worshipping the One True God, Allah. Staying connected to God and repenting from mistakes and sins is the road to salvation.

The concept of a Trinity--Father, Son, and Holy Spirit--is firmly rejected for there is but one God.

26

Hindus and Buddhists

Hindus and Buddhists are two faiths which are in many ways very similar. We will consider Hindu first.

Hindus are impressive for their unlimited tolerance and nonjudgmental recognition of other religions as all being equal. Hindu is equally known for its myths, asceticism, meditation (yoga) and amazing variety of gods and holy opinions, all of which are equally accepted even when they disagree or contradict each other. Who is to know, so who is to say?

Hinduism is really more a philosophy than a religion in that it does not believe in heaven, hell, salvation, redemption, or eternal life. They do believe that in death we enter a state of "eternal bliss," in which there is an end to all suffering. We remain in this state until we are reincarnated, which is when the spiritual soul is reunited in the physical realm with a new body. This reincarnation can happen a number of times as the soul learns and grows each time. This cycle is called "samsara."

Reincarnation in Hinduism is not limited to being born as human. You may have had prior lives as animals, plants, or as divine beings who rule part of nature. If it has life, then it is part of the cycle of reincarnation. Remember that the next time you step on and crush a bug. According to the idea of reincarnation, it could be your great-uncle or future grandchild!

Karma, a well know Hindu term, is the belief that if we achieve good deeds in this life it will contribute to the quality of the next life. Ahimsa, not as well known, is to practice nonviolence to all living things. If followed, ahimsa will help you attain good karma, which in turn will help achieve a higher quality in the next life.

The ultimate goal of the Hindu is to achieve union with the eternal soul, Brahman. This can be attained through meditation, yoga, and devotion to one's duty. This highest state is called "nirvana," union with the universe and release from the cycle of death and rebirth and reincarnation.

The well-known caste system in Indian culture was created by Krishna, who is a major deity considered by most believers to be the eighth incarnation of Vishnu. He, or sometimes she, is perhaps the most popular of all the heroes of Hindu mythology.

Krishna's main duty is to help people to keep focusing on their duty and to teach them to be dispassionate about life, not to seek material things or social advancement, because attachment to worldly objects is superficial and leads only to suffering in the end.

In Hindu there are thirty-three gods, but three who really matter: Brahma the creator, Vishnu the preserver, and Shiva the destroyer. These three make up the Trimurti which has no comparison with the Christian Trinity except the number three.

Differences from Christian Faith

Hinduism is a very congenial and non-competitive religion in which everyone and everything is always right because there is no wrong! It doesn't matter therefore what you believe or even if you believe. Unlike Christianity, Hinduism believes ultimately nothing matters, it will all come again and you will be here again as well. So relax and enjoy life.

In the Hindu faith, Jesus has been given a place in the pantheon of holiness alongside Krishna, Rama, Isvara, Purusha and other more minor divinities. But since Hindu assimilated Jesus as only one of the many holy prophets, Christians must give up their claim to Jesus being the one and only savior of the world. Hindus will accept Jesus as a yogi or guru, as one avatar among many incarnations of the divine reality, but that's all.

The Hindu have 4 holy books, called the Veda. The Veda is very much like the Hebrew Bible, in being a collection of religious texts. It includes mythological accounts, poems, prayers, and formulas considered to be sacred but not regarded as binding upon believers. The Veda was composed in India between about 1500 and 1000 B.C.

Buddhism

Buddhism is in many ways comparative to Hindu. It is impressive as a kind of middle way between materialism and secularism on the one hand, and self-denial or a monastic lifestyle on the other. Buddha says life is and must be a little of both, so take both as they come and give yourself to neither. Buddhism says suffering is self-inflicted; it comes as the consequences of our pride, greed, and selfish actions. One can move above selfishness and pride by willpower and self-determination. And one must rise above it, because he must progress in this life in order to gain another life, and each successive life must be better than the past one. The goal of each life is to be less materialistic, less judgmental, and more loving and spiritual than in the previous life.

Buddhism takes nothing seriously, "This too will pass" is their view about everything; it is not important in the long run, so just meditate it away. The goal as you move through each successive life is to be untouched by anything except pure enlightenment. The ultimate ambition and goal is to attain Buddhahood, which is perfect enlightenment, in which all things are known and understood with wisdom and compassion.

The Buddhist faith has a kind of trinity called the Triple Gem, composed of the Buddha, the Dharma, and the Sangha. It also has something very close to the Ten Commandments, called the Ten Meritorious Deeds:

Not to kill
Not to steal
Not to commit adultery
Not to lie
Not to gossip

Not to say cruel and hurtful words
Not to speak beguiling words
Not to be greedy
Not to hate
Not to deny the existence of past lives and future lives

Differences from Christian Faith

Buddhists have 5 holy books: the Pali Canon, the Sanskrit Canon, the Mahayana texts, the Tantric texts, and the Tibetan and Mongolian Canon. These texts tell of the holy law by which believers ought to live. Some teach how to obtain spirituality and some relate the lives and deeds of the main historical figures in the faith.

The sacred texts can be read or understood in a variety of different ways: as the unchanging "Word of God" to be taken literally and applied directly to life, or as being metaphorical or poetic. For many, they are the instruction and guide for how to live a life that is pleasing to the Buddha.

Zen Buddhism does not use texts at all but relies completely on meditation to connect directly with God.

Like Hinduism, Buddhism is an unhistorical religion. That is, both care nothing at all for history and have no interest in creation. Buddhism sees everything as a circle of repetition. It has all happened before and will happen again. History and life repeat themselves; so don't take them seriously, just go with it.

For both Hindu and Buddha religions, everything has been predetermined and we simply walk through the plan. Nothing we do can change the plan for our lives, since it has all been determined. Thus, quiescence and apathy are characteristics of both religions; simply turn the other cheek and do not get involved.

Buddhists are always open to discuss things of the spirit. They reinterpret the message of Jesus in the light of their own understanding of the teachings of Buddha, and doing that, we find there are many comparisons and some differences.

They agree Jesus is the Christ, the anointed one just as Gautama is the Buddha, the enlightened one. But the truths of Buddha's teachings are not tied to the person of Gautama himself in the same way the Gospel is tied to Jesus. For Christianity, salvation depends upon what God has done in the historical Jesus, the flesh and blood man whose humanity and divinity bridge the gap between human beings and God. Not so Buddha, who is merely someone who has a better grasp of enlightened truth than anyone else.

The big difference between Christianity, Hinduism and Buddhism is the twisted agony of Jesus on the cross contrasted to the smiling fat Buddha sitting on a lotus blossom, or the calm countenance of a Hindu knowing everything is an illusion and in the end doesn't matter.

The crucified Christ testifies to the presence of evil and failure, rejection and hate that is the sin of this world. Buddha simply shrugs and says you can rise above all these things by meditation and giving yourself to the pursuit of peace. Hindu says just smile and it will all go away.

For both Hindus and Buddhists, if you have good humor, tranquility and peace will come. And if not, you will have another chance in another life.

27

Mormons

I have placed Mormons (Latter-day Saints) into the category of "other faiths;" because while Mormons insist they are Christian, if that claim is judged by its stipulated beliefs, it is difficult to see how this claim is true. To my eyes, so much in the Mormon faith is unrecognizable as bearing any similarity to the Christian faith.

And yet, it must be strongly admitted that without question, Mormonism has much to recommend it to its adherents with much of good will and good work within it. Whether it can be considered Christian is highly debatable.

In 1830 Joseph Smith said he saw God and Jesus Christ in a vision after praying to know which church to join. In that vision God and Jesus both called on him not to join a church but to restore the church Christ had organized when He was on earth, but which had become corrupted and was a failure. Smith was to rebuild the church, this time with the proper organization and priesthood authority that that had been lost shortly after the Savior's death.

Then, in the fall of 1823, Smith was led by an angel named Maroni to a place not far from the Smith farm near Palmyra, New York, where Maroni had buried gold-colored plates fourteen hundred years earlier. Smith said they were writings of ancient Hebrews who had migrated from Israel to the Americas.

Smith claimed the plates were written in a lost reformed Egyptian language which he was able to translate with the help of "seer stones" believed at the time to be a means by which to receive divine revelations. He alone could read the language, but he dictated what they said to a scribe and then published the tablets as the Book of Mormon. The Angel Maroni took the plates from Smith after they had been translated and returned them to heaven.

The Mormons accept the Christian Bible but the Book of Mormon has equal importance and reverence. In Mormonism God is not the only god; there are multiple gods, living on multiple planets, even though the only "gods' in the pantheon to be worshipped are God the Father, Jesus and the Holy Spirit.

The multiple gods of Mormonism is a doctrine not generally known because Mormons identify themselves as Christians; and traditional Christianity affirms, with Islam and Judaism, that there is but one God.

Mormonism states that all human beings lived with God as spirits before being born and came to earth to receive physical bodies in order to learn and grow. It also maintains that the mind or the intelligence which human beings possess is coequal with God himself. The mind is also immortal because it has no beginning or ending.

For Mormons, while the death of Christ redeems all people from the sin of Adam, his death does not cover our own personal sins. Those must be dealt with through faith, church involvement and faithful service to the Lord. Each of us must do all we can to live a proper life and then trust in the mercy of God. The Church exists to help us become worthy of God's blessings.

Mormons refer to the Trinity as "the Godhead" but believe the three members of the Trinity are three physically separate beings, but one in love, purpose, and will. God the father has a human-like body but is immortal and perfected. Jesus, the only perfect man who ever lived, set the example in His life for all to follow. Because humans fall short, Christ's atoning sacrifice pays the price of sin on condition of individual repentance. His sacrifice also allows all humankind to be resurrected into immortality. In that sense he is the Savior.

Latter-day Saints believe The Holy Spirit (they prefer "Holy Ghost") can inspire and influence righteous people who are receptive to those promptings. The "gift" of the Holy Ghost is given after baptism to members of the Church by a priesthood holder, who puts his hands on the head of the baptized person and blesses him or her to "receive the Holy Ghost." This grants the privilege of enjoying the Holy Ghost's constant companionship if God's commandments are followed.

Mormons maintain the New Testament church is full of errors and falsehoods and was in need of Joseph Smith and the Book of Mormon to correct it. They maintain that the ecumenical councils of the church, which produced the Nicene Creed and the Apostles Creed, are all false understandings which contradict scripture as amended by the book of Mormon.

Mormonism is a religion among religions, and the inclusion of Jesus Christ in its name does not make it part of the Christian faith.

28

Atheism...Agnosticism...Secularism

Atheism and agnosticism are in many ways two sides of the same coin. Atheism asserts, somewhat philosophically, that God does not exist, and that religion is a projection of human need and fantasy, created because of human weakness.

Agnosticism is the term for those who are not sure there is a God, but who cannot go as far as atheism and completely deny that God exists. What they mean is that they just do not know whether there is a God or not.

Okay, but think for a moment, that doesn't work either. There really is no such middle ground. Either there is a God or there is not. If you don't believe there is a God, then you believe there is not a God. It's one or the other. My mother always told me, "You can't have your cake and eat it too."

Secularism is something else entirely. Generally

speaking, secularism is not so much a religious view. It simply promotes living according to whatever viewpoint makes sense to you; that is, if you bother to even think about it, which you do not need to do. Just live, baby!

I wonder how much of the increase in drugs, violence, and suicide in recent years in the United States is simply due to our being increasingly a society that denies the reality of God, denies any personal meaning to life and thus to each person's own life. This is a philosophy which ultimately leaves them basically worthless individuals, living in an empty nothing.

I don't know how you do that...how you deny as nothing every good deed we witness, every beautiful thing we see, every experience of love in our lives. To have the love of a wife, or husband, or child, and to say this is nice to have, but ultimately meaningless. Man, it takes a great faith to believe that!

Psychology tells us everyone must have what is called an integrating principle in their lives, a core or base position or belief which tells us who we are. We must have that, which means that in one way or another we will choose something in which to believe. Even atheists and agnostics and secularists must believe in something! It might be crystals or the ethnic superiority of Germans, the magic power of kiwi, or whatever. Any of those beliefs can, at least to some extent, integrate you.

But to say with the atheists, "I don't believe God exists," or to say with the agnostics, "I don't know if God exists," or to say with the secularists, "I don't care whether God exists," is to push God out of the core of your being.

The differences from the Christian Faith are obvious:

1. Atheism simply denies the existence of God and therefore the value of the Christian faith or any other religious point of view.

2. Agnosticism equivocates about what it believes or does not believe to the point of becoming atheism by default.

3. Secularism, beyond making commercial use of Christian Holy Days (Christmas and Easter) has no interest in the Christian faith. It is well on the way to doing the same with Islam, and then who or what will be next?

29

LGBTQ

LGBTQ is not a religion or an aspect of religion and those who identify with this grouping may be members of any religious view, or of none.

However, this is a book on the Christian faith and what the Christian faith says about those who identify as lesbian, gay, bisexual, transgender, queer or questioning (LGBTQ), is of concern to any person who shares the faith.

I am dealing with it only because it is unfortunately an issue filled with anger, misunderstanding and fearfulness. The Christian Faith is often quoted and misquoted in regard to LGBTQ to such an extent it is difficult to comment on it in a careful and honest manner. But, if you stay with me, I will attempt to do that.

To begin, we must acknowledge, without in any way agreeing with the position, that there are some within the Christian Church who regard those within the LGBTQ community as clearly and without question living in sin. Some even go to the extreme and say, without support anywhere in the Christian faith, that it is unforgiveable sin.

Those in the church who oppose LGBTQ generally do so by quoting various passages in the Bible. For example, Leviticus says, "It is an abomination for a man to lie with a man as with a woman." (Lev. 18:22; 20:13). In Romans 1 Paul condemns homosexuality of either men or women as "unnatural and dishonorable."

For some, that is clear enough to end the matter. But there are real problems with doing that. The first problem is that we live in the 21st Century, and those passages come from the 1st Century and centuries earlier. Leviticus, Romans, and other such passages must be read within the culture and the context of the time in which they were written. We cannot read forward the understanding of an earlier age and apply it to this age.

I say this even though, as I write at the end of 2020, all around the country statues are being torn down, reputations being shattered, because someone who lived 100 or 200 years ago did not share current understandings and values. This is sad, verging on stupid, and only those with no sense or understanding of history can demand that previous centuries have the same cultural understanding the present century does.

That's the first problem. Culture "then" was different from now and that fact simply cannot be ignored as if it didn't matter. It matters totally. We cannot require a past culture to have the same insights and understanding as one 2,500 years later in time.

The second problem is that when we take the Bible as a whole, it actually has very little to say about LGBTQ or homosexuality in any manner. It is not mentioned in the Ten Commandments. Jesus never said a word about it; and in the early church, it was a matter of hardly any, if any, importance to faith.

The Talmud, a 1st Century commentary on the Jewish Scripture (Old Testament) says, "We do not see things as they are, we see things as we are." That's a good description of the sinful inclination in all of us. In this context it means that we must come to the Bible looking for what God has to say, not looking for support for what we want it to say.

Ah, but that immediately becomes a question of how we are to properly read and understand the Bible! (For a more detailed answer to this question, I refer you to my book, "*Then is Now: Reading the New Testament in the 21st Century.*"

To answer that question here, briefly put, the Bible is not a book composed of eternal truths which are applicable to all times and situations, and therefore to be taken literally and applied directly to life. It is a book which must be interpreted bearing in mind both the context in which it was written, and the context in which it is being read.

Much of scripture IS conditioned by the cultural situation existing at the time it was written; and in order to understand it correctly, we must read it within that context. Often scripture records the word of God addressed to a particular situation, and we cannot take what is said to that situation and apply it to a totally different one.

The context and the culture determine the meaning of what is said; and when applied in a different context or different culture, the meaning may very well change. This is a fundamental principle of biblical interpretation.

For example, we do not directly apply scripture to our lives when it says that if a woman has sexual intercourse during certain times of the month she shall be put to death, or when it says that if a person is divorced they cannot marry again, or that Christians must not lend money at interest!

Even those who would agree with Leviticus that *"it is an abomination for a man to lie with a man as with a woman"* would surely not equally agree with Leviticus a few verses later when it says, *"If a man does lie with a man as with a woman, they shall both be put to death"* or *"If a son curses his father he shall be put to death."*

When we insist the Bible is to be taken as it is written and not interpreted on the basis of the culture of the times, we have some difficult decisions to make! Read literally, the Bible says some things that make our hair stand on end!

Jesus condemned the Pharisees for their narrow interpretation of scripture, and we are always in danger of falling into the same error and focusing so closely on the few passages that speak about homosexuality, that we forget what the Bible says about the whole human condition.

Much more is said about the foibles and loves of human beings…about the saint and sinner in us all…about the forgiveness and new life that is possible for those who are baptized into the resurrection of Jesus Christ...and how we are to emulate Jesus and seek to love one another as we are loved.

It is the main point and central thrust of Scripture, to say that in Jesus Christ we have the full and complete revelation of God's will not only for human life but for all cosmic existence. And it clearly says, from the first page to the last, that anything...any opinion, any attitude, any behavior, anything which degrades, enslaves or belittles another person... is not only against the will of God, but is born of Evil.

More than anything else, it is the point of Scripture to tell us that God so loves the world and all his human children, all of them, that he gave his only Son, so that we might not be condemned, but brought to life and salvation.

And what needs to be clarified in the discussion with those who consider LGBTQ to be a sin is exactly what it is that is sinful about it. And if it is a sin, what is there is about it that makes it so much more sinful than other sins?

Personally, I can't think of anything. But then I don't consider it a sin anyhow.

Let me end this way: every generation of the church has had to wrestle with some tough, sometimes terrible, and often frightful questions. And every time the living reality of the Holy Spirit calls us out from ourselves and our own desires, gathers us into the fellowship of Christ, enlightens us with his presence, and preserves the church, and us, in true faith. So it has been. So it will be regarding the LGBTQ community as well.

Reprise

A very brief restatement of this book

Creation, life, and the end of life are all in the hands of God who made the world, every day sustains it, and in his time will bring it all to an end.

However, this same God raised Jesus from the dead as an indication of his intention for human life and creation: that it will not simply end in destruction but in rebirth and new life.

The Bible tells us repeatedly that things are not as they appear, that human history is not simply a linear progression from the past to the future; but that while we exist under the forms of time and space, through God's act in Christ we have been freed from the confines of time and space.

Even now, while still in the body, we are living a resurrected life. The kingdom of God has come among us, wrapped itself around us and redeemed us. We have been saved. St. Paul says, *"If we live, we live in the Lord, if we die, we die in the Lord. So whether we live or whether we die, we are the Lord's."* (Romans 14:8)

We are already living in the Spirit even though a time of consummation is still to come. A banquet, as Jesus put it, of which we have so far tasted only the appetizer.

Banquets, streets of gold, blood on the moon, beasts, and fiery pits...it's all in the Bible and it's all symbolic language. We can't take it literally. The Bible speaks in symbolic language because that's the only language in which we can describe such things. Whether we are Daniel or Einstein, symbols are all we have in which to capture reality. Especially eternal reality.

Try to conceive of a time when time was not...it's as impossible as it is to conceive of a time when time will no longer be. It's beyond our ability because we are involved in it even as we seek to understand it. St. Augustine once said, "If nobody asks me what time is, I understand it perfectly, but as soon as I am asked to explain it, I become completely confused."

We make a mistake when we treat symbolic language as if it were literal description; because, in doing that, we grab hold of the surface meaning but miss the deeper part. We get the frosting but not the cake, and we never know if it's chocolate, white, or marble. And you can get sick on only frosting! When we take things literally, we miss the truth to which the literal words merely bear witness.

So also, to think of the resurrection of Jesus, of resurrected life, as merely unending time, is to grab the surface and miss the depth. Resurrected life is a whole different dimension.

It's not a matter of quantity, but quality. The eternal life of which Jesus speaks is something which begins now and is lived here and now, a "foretaste" of the future, which will come to completion only when it is perfected by God at the end of time.

Christians still have to die, but death changes its meaning when you know you have already tasted of that which lies beyond death's door. Our self, who we are, our love, whom we love, will all be there when we awaken from the "big sleep."

Until then we live in a tension between this world, in which the glory of God is veiled and the righteousness of God seems compromised, and the world to come, where the whole meaning of life and history will be revealed as the accomplishment of God's purposes.

But all of that is so huge it can only be symbolized.

We can only try to describe the indescribable and realize that when we do, the result will be more the product of our limited understanding than anything else. We can't know what is yet to be.

Still, by faith we can know, utterly and certainly, that in the midst of all that is and ever will be, we are held tightly within the love of the Almighty God of creation who bids us call him Father. And we can know that all things are within his power. And that on that day to come, whenever, whatever, however, we shall be with God in a way that fulfills and completes the intention he has had, Peter says, "from before the foundation of the world."

The other side of heaven is hell. Not so much a literal place as a way of saying that dying is inevitable, but arriving at the perfection God desires for human life is not inevitable, and it is possible to get lost along the road and never arrive at the intended destination.

The non-Christian religions of the world are neither wrong nor misguided. They are vehicles of God's revelation and grace; and in whatever way God chooses, they will become a path to fulfillment in Jesus Christ…someday, some way. We are all brothers and sisters in God's grace and love, and we are all redeemed and forgiven in Christ's death and resurrection.

Secularism and its partner atheism, on the other hand, are badly misguided. And we need to say to them that God offers his grace and forgiveness to all his children in the world. And it really does matter whether or not we accept it.

Jesus Christ has been raised from death, and through him God brings fulfillment to all life and creation. Today, tomorrow, and every day to come, the grace and love of God is there for us. But if you don't know it, you can't have it. And that matters a great deal.

                     Solei Deo Gloria

About the Author

Wayne R Viereck is a Pastor of the Evangelical Lutheran Church in America. After graduation from the University of Wisconsin with a degree in English and History, he followed with a Master of Divinity degree from the Lutheran School of Theology in Chicago and subsequently pursued a Master of Sacred Theology degree at the same school. He concluded his formal studies with a Doctor of Ministry degree from LSTC, which was awarded with distinction.

Pastor Viereck has served as a parish pastor for 59 years during which time he led numerous discussions of the New Testament, church history and theology. In these classes he encountered an insatiable and boundless hunger for a lay-oriented understanding of the Christian faith.

The acclaimed author of "Then is Now: Reading the New Testament in the 21st Century," Dr. Viereck attempts in this new book to respond to those many requests, for a readable approach to understanding the Christian Faith in terms of the 21st Century world.

It is offered with thankful appreciation for the many amazing people within and without the congregations he has served, who in living their faith, have taught him what faith is...and what the Christian Faith is truly all about.

To them be the thanks...to God be the Glory!

Made in the USA
Las Vegas, NV
26 December 2022

64223168R00118